D0208454

Birder's Dictionary

Randall T. Cox

FALCON

Helena, Montana

BIRDER'S DICTIONARY
By Randall T. Cox

Falcon Press is continually expanding its list of books. You can order extra copies
of this book and get information and prices for other Falcon books by writing
Falcon Press, P.O. Box 1718, Helena, MT 59624 or calling 1-800-582-2665. Please
ask for a free copy of our current catalog listing all Falcon Press books.

Copyright © 1996 by Falcon Press Publishing Co., Inc.

Helena and Billings, Montana

All rights reserved, including the right to reproduce this book or parts thereof, in
any form, except for the inclusion of brief quotations in a review.

Printed in Canada.

Falcon Press Publishing Co., Inc.
P.O. Box 1718
Helena, MT 59624

Illustrations by Todd Telander

Cover photo: © Jerry & Barbara Jividen, Images Unique Photography
The Sibley - Ahlquist - Monroe (SAM) Classification System in Appendix IV is
reprinted from Proctor and Lynch, <u>Manual of Ornithology</u>, pp. 308-317.
Copyright © Yale University Press, New Haven, CT. Permission granted.

 Text pages printed on recycled paper.

ISBN 1-56044-423-1

Library of Congress Cataloging-in-Publication Data

Cox, Randall, T., 1951-
    Birder's dictionary / Randall T. Cox
        p.   cm.
    Includes bibliographical references.
    ISBN 1-56044-423-1 (pbk. : alk. paper)
    1. Ornithology—Dictionaries. 2. Birds—Dictionaries. I. Title.
QL672.2.C69
598'.03—dc20   96-15363
                                                        CIP

This book is dedicated in memory of
Edward Avery McIlhenny and my grandmother,
Florence Taylor McIlhenny, for their acute
interest in birds and for inspiring my own.

External Anatomy
(Blue Jay)

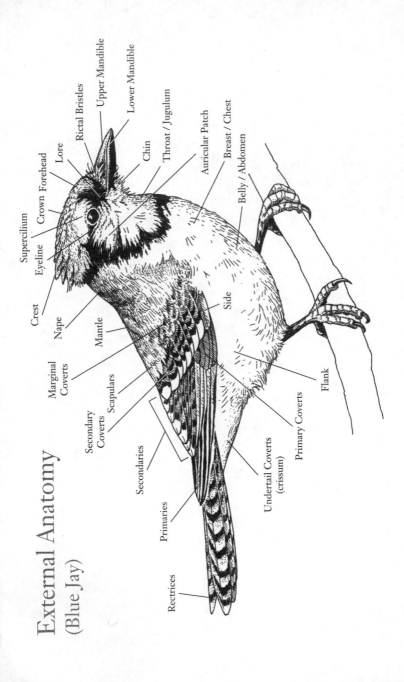

Supercilium
Crown Forehead
Lore
Rictal Bristles
Upper Mandible
Lower Mandible
Chin
Throat / Jugulum
Auricular Patch
Breast / Chest
Belly / Abdomen
Eyeline
Crest
Nape
Mantle
Side
Marginal Coverts
Scapulars
Secondary Coverts
Secondaries
Flank
Primaries
Undertail Coverts (crissum)
Primary Coverts
Rectrices

ACKNOWLEDGMENTS

I gratefully acknowledge the work of my wife, Kate Missett, whose able editing contributed enormously to this endeavor; Bradley Crompton, graduate student in zoology, University of Wyoming, for his valued technical review; and Greg Butcher and Gus Daniels of the American Birding Association, for spotting errors. My special appreciation goes to Dr. Philip Wright, my ornithology professor in 1974, now professor emeritus of ornithology and zoology, University of Montana, for editing and putting details into context, especially for suggestions regarding classification and taxonomy. Our gratitude is also due to the Denver Museum of Natural History for their help with the illustrations. Skilled typing by my cheerful assistant, Shirley Carton, several times saved me from chucking the project and going insane. Responsibility for all errors and omissions rests with the author. I welcome comments, corrections, and suggestions for improvements from any sources.

–Randall Cox is an avid birder and naturalist who has lived in northeast Wyoming most of his life. He practices law, emphasizing water rights and environmental law, in Wyoming and Montana.

CONTENTS

PREFACE

Why a birder's dictionary? Birds and bird watching are enormously popular. Amateurs, professionals, artists, conservationists, children, outdoors enthusiasts, travelers, hunters, casual observers, and fanatics alike are fascinated by avifauna. The thousands of published books and monographs about birds occupy a healthy chunk of shelf space in nearly every bookstore. Today's birding magazines have an explosive popularity. Shops that feature birding gear and bird-feeding supplies appear in most malls. Even bird tours, sold as an upscale form of adventure, are increasing.

Why add to the profusion by writing *Birder's Dictionary*? Among the varied titles published about birds are several excellent reference works (listed in this book's bibliography), but these are large and expensive. Except for four large encyclopedias, the available bird books lack comprehensive glossaries. Since most birders haven't the time to enroll in a college ornithology course or search lengthy texts for a definition, their sources are often limited to field guides and a common dictionary, inadequate tools.

Based in part upon these—my own—frustrations, I perceived a need for a comprehensive dictionary of "bird words" that is not only complete and compact, but also easy to understand and use. Most birders and students are not familiar with anatomical and biological terminology, so my goal was to provide definitions in plain English. Cross references and parallel references are provided, but nearly all of the definitions in this book are designed to stand on their own.

A birder's field dictionary should fit in a day pack or a glove box. I hope that guests on bird tours and cruises will keep a copy of *Birder's Dictionary* in their pockets or cabins, that parents will use the book to answer children's questions, that students will carry it to the laboratory and field, and that ornithology professors will find it convenient to refresh memories and answer questions. Some people might even sit down and read it cover to cover.

INTRODUCTION

This dictionary-style reference work is complete enough to be a valuable aid to zoologists, but it was designed primarily to be easy for beginners to carry, use, and understand.

Like any list of bird-related definitions, *Birder's Dictionary* contains many entries regarding avian anatomy, including birds' internal structure and function, external structure and function, and appearance. It goes into great detail about feathers, which are anatomical features unique to birds. However, since it is a general reference work for use by amateurs as well as professionals, it does not include anatomical minutiae—the names of individual muscles, nerves, blood vessels, and feather tracts. Birders who seek this kind of information should refer to one of the more encyclopedic texts listed in the bibliography or the primary literature, scientific journals about birds.

In addition to anatomy, this book lists properties and behaviors regarding bird metabolism and physiology. Examples include digestion, reproduction, and body heat regulation. *Birder's Dictionary* provides comprehensive definitions of general metabolic, physiologic, and reproductive biology without delving into many details of specialized subjects such as cell biology and genetics.

This easy-to-use dictionary also includes descriptive terms regarding avian behavior. Birds exhibit many unusual types of display, courtship, mating, nesting, rearing, feeding, hygienic, and other behaviors (for example, the practice of "anting"). Evolution, especially of birds, contains mysteries that will fascinate professors and *Jurassic Park* fans forever. Any discussion of the origins and divergence of bird groups, from orders to races, is one of relationships and processes. The entries in this text include many details regarding classification (relationships) and general information regarding evolutionary processes.

Terms pertaining to broader fields of biology and zoology also are defined here, when convenient, with specific reference to birds. Readers are invited to send comments about definitions and suggestions for additional terms to the publisher. All suggested corrections and amplifications will be gratefully considered. Both publisher and author welcome stories about uses of this dictionary ("My kids love it," "It's handy for propping up a camp stove," "I impressed everyone on the Galapagos tour," etc.) and may include these in future editions as well.

Taxonomy, Classification, and Names

This dictionary also includes terms dealing with taxonomy, or the classification and naming of birds, a complex and controversial subject. All birds are of the taxonomic class Aves. The class is divided into orders, which in turn are divided into families, then into genera (plural of genus), then into individual species. Taxonomists also use intermediate groupings such as suborders, tribes, and superfamilies.

Drawing a bold line between taxonomic terms to be included and terms to be excluded is impossible. Scientific, English, and colloquial names are used liberally throughout the text. Although scientists justifiably question inclusion of colloquial names in reference works, such names are a useful way for many people to find information, especially if they are not familiar with accepted taxonomic usage.

Just what is "accepted taxonomic usage" is the subject of great controversy among professional ornithologists; witness the changes between the editions of the official *Check-list of North American Birds* published by the American Ornithologists' Union (AOU). Many birds that were listed as separate species in earlier editions of the *Check-list* were lumped as races of single species in the Sixth Edition (1983), but are likely to be split again into separate species in the Seventh Edition. The powerful AOU Committee on Classification and Nomenclature continues its deliberations; lumpers and splitters will likely never come to peaceful ends.

Meanwhile, Charles Sibley and Burt Monroe, eminent

ornithologists (and past presidents of the AOU), have devised their own world checklist of birds based upon DNA similarities and other features. The Sibley-Ahlquist-Monroe (SAM) Classification System of infraclasses, parvclasses, superorders, orders, suborders, infraorders, families, genera, and species differs widely from the classifications employed in the *AOU Check-lists*, and is likely to influence avian taxonomy for many years.

Within *Birder's Dictionary*, varieties of these lists of bird groups are provided in several appendices. Those who simply wish to look up a family name and see generally to which birds it refers can turn to an alphabetical list of North American families, Appendix I. Appendices II and III comprise, respectively, all North American and world bird orders and families, organized systematically in accordance with the *AOU Check-list*, Sixth Edition (1983). A separate appendix (Appendix IV) lists bird orders and subgroupings in accordance with the SAM classification system (1990), which reorganizes bird classification on the basis of DNA similarities.

Other Sources of Information

Information for this book came from a wide variety of sources, from Robert Ridgway's 1887 *Manual of the Birds of North America* to the books listed in the bibliography, and from Webster's Unabridged Dictionary to many other texts and monographs. Since some of the leading encyclopedias and ornithology textbooks provide excellent in-depth discussions and illustrations of topics for those seeking more details, cross references to selected publications are included within term definitions. Most of these books are fairly expensive but should be available at public or university libraries. (The computerized inter-library loan system can access libraries nationwide with astonishing success. I owe a huge debt to the reference staff at the public library in Gillette, Wyoming, for finding out-of-print books in government, university, and small libraries scattered from Wisconsin to Texas.) The bibliography at the end of the text lists these and other references.

Information about government publications or updates may be obtained by contacting the National Biological Service centers at the following addresses:

National Biological Service Center
4512 McMurry Avenue
Fort Collins, CO 80525-3400

8711 37th Street SE.
Jamestown, ND 58401-7317
e-mail: Kirsten_Lahlum@nbs.gov

12100 Beech Forest Road
Laurel, MD 20708-4039
e-mail: Lynda_Garrett@nbs.gov

900 Clay Street,
Vicksburg, MS 39180

Ken Reinecke in Vicksburg can send a list of more than 6,700 references to the ecology of waterfowl if you send him two 1.4Mb floppy disks and a postage-paid envelope. The data come in compressed form; readers will need decompressing software. Internet buffs can find National Biological Survey data on the World Wide Web at http: //www.nbs.gov.

Those seeking other bird books are encouraged to see *Birding* magazine, published by the American Birding Association (ABA), which also publishes periodic catalogs. The ABA may be contacted at P.O. Box 6599, Colorado Springs, CO 80934; (800) 634-7736. Current and out-of-print books also are offered periodically by Buteo Books, Route 1, Box 242, Shipman, VA 22971; (804) 263-8671.

Aa

ABA, American Birding Association, P.O. Box 6599, Colorado Springs, Colorado 80934.

AOU, American Ornithologists' Union, c/o Ornithological Societies of North America, P.O. Box 1897, Lawrence, Kansas 66044-8897.

abdomen, *n.*, the lower part of the ventral (front) exterior surface of a bird, below the breast and above the cloaca (vent), also termed the belly; **[field mark].** *See illustration, p. v.*

abdominal, *adj.*, pertaining to the abdomen.

abductor, *adj.*, describing muscles that pull away from the center of the body or an appendage (for example, muscles used in the upstroke of wings during flight); opposite of **adductor**.

abundant, *adj.*, denoting species frequently sighted in their home range, winter range, breeding grounds, or migration staging areas.

accidental, *adj.*, describing birds that occasionally stray from their normal ranges or migration routes and who do not breed regularly or occur annually in a given geographic area (for example, western North America).

accipiter, any member of the hawk genus *Accipiter*, medium-sized to large hawks with long tails, short rounded wings, rapid flight, rapid wingbeats alternating with short glides, and aggressive hunting techniques (for example, Northern Goshawk, *Accipiter gentilis*).

accipitral, *adj.*, see **accipitrine**.

accipitrine, *adj.*, of or like an accipiter (bird of prey); same as **accipitral**.

1

acetabulum, *n.*, the cup-shaped socket in the pelvic girdle (hip) into which the femur (thighbone) fits.

acicular, *adj.*, needle-shaped, acute.

aculeate, *adj.*, slender and pointed.

acuminate, *adj.*, tapering gradually to a point; contrast with **attenuate**

acute, *adj.*, describes a bill that tapers to a sharp point (for example, the bill of a warbler [*Parulinae*]); opposite of **obtuse.**

adaptive radiation, *n.*, the evolutionary process of adapting to fill new ecological/biological niches (for example, Darwin's finches: several species, each adapted to different conditions, "radiated" from a common ancestor); same as **divergent evolution**; see also **genetic drift**.

addled, *adj.*, describing an egg that is empty or rotten.

adductor, *adj.*, describing muscles used to draw toward the center of the body or an appendage (for example, muscles to close jaws, strong in hawks and seed-crushing birds); opposite of **abductor**.

adherent, *adj.*, describing coloration of plumage by external agents; see **adventitious**.

adrenal cortex, *n.*, the part of the adrenal glands that secretes metabolic regulators or steroid hormones.

adult, *n.*, an individual of maturity, typically with definitive plumage and breeding capability.

adventitious, *adj.*, changed color in plumage caused by environmental factors (for example, iron oxide causing reddening of plumage of Sandhill Cranes); same as **adherent**.

aerie, *n.*, the nest of a hawk, eagle, falcon, or osprey, high on a tree or cliff, see also **eyrie**.

afterfeather, *n.*, a supplemental small feather springing from the base of a contour feather, thought to provide additional insulation, common in grouse; same as **hypoptile**.

aftershaft, *n.*, the shaft of an afterfeather or hypoptile; same as **hyporachis**.

aggression, *n.*, threatening, attack, or combat behavior; see also Campbell & Lack, pp. 7-9.

agonistic, *adj.*, describing aggressive behavior or posturing, short of actual combat.

air sacs, *n.*, a series of thin-walled "bubbles" situated among the lungs and bones and other internal organs. The air sacs allow unidirectional flow through the lungs (which enhances respiration efficiency), provide cooling, produce pressure that allows for vocalization, and serve other functions.

alar, *adj.*, pertaining to the wing.

alaudine, *adj.*, larklike.

albescence, *n.*, an abnormal condition of plumage characterized by albinism and looseness or hairiness of feather structure.

albinism, *n.*, color variation caused by an absence or reduction of pigments in feathers, including four types: **total albinism**, in which all pigments are completely absent from feathers, skin, and irises; **incomplete albinism**, in which pigment is absent from one or more of the feathers, skin, or irises, but not all three; **imperfect albinism**, in which all pigments are reduced or at least one pigment is missing; and **partial albinism**, the most common form in birds, in which pigments are reduced or absent from parts of the feathers, skin, or irises; see also **melanism**; see also Campbell & Lack, pp. 472-4.

albinistic, *adj.*, describes a bird deficient in pigmentation; see **albinism**, **albino**.

albino, *n.*, an animal with deficient pigmentation; see **albinism**.

albumen, *n.*, the "white" of the egg, which supplies water and protein to the developing embryo and also provides a buffer against shock and heat loss.

alcid, family name for the auks, razorbills, murres, puffins, and guillemots (*Alcidae*).

aliform, *adj.*, wing-like.

alimentary canal, *n.*; see **alimentary system**.

alimentary system, *n.*, the digestive system from the beak to the vent, including the bill, caeca, cloaca, colon, crop (if present), duodenum, esophagus, ileum, mouth, proventriculus, salivary glands, secretory glands, tongue, and ventriculus; also termed the **alimentary canal;** see also Campbell & Lack, pp. 10-12.

allantois, *n.*, a membranous system in embryonic development, within the egg, which provides for respiration and storage of metabolic wastes in the form of insoluble urates; see also **amnion**, **chorion**.

Allen's Rule, *n.*, a rule of adaptation to environment which says that bills, tails, and other extensions of the body tend to be longer in warmer climates and shorter in cooler climates; see also **Bergmann's Rule**.

allopatric, *adj.*, describing two species (often two highly similar species) whose breeding ranges do not overlap and who generally do not interbreed or hybridize. Together the two species are called a superspecies (for example, Western and Eastern Meadowlarks); contrast with **sympatric**, a condition where ranges do overlap.

allopatric speciation, *n.*, the evolution of separate species from a common ancestor following a period of separation and isolation, particularly in "virgin" habitats (those not inhabited by other species with similar requirements).

allopreening, *n.*, the practice by one individual, usually a mate, of preening another individual, more often observed at the nest or in captivity. Also an agonistic display in many species (for example, macaws, birds of prey). Practiced by many species.

allospecies, *n.*, members of a superspecies. If two highly similar species occupy overlapping ranges but do not interbreed or hybridize frequently, they are considered to be members of a superspecies; if they interbreed frequently, they are considered to be members of different subspecies of the same species. Drawing these distinctions can be controversial.

alpine, *adj.*, pertaining to the Alps or any high mountain range and describing species inhabiting such high altitudes.

alternate, *adj.*, describing nonbasic plumage in birds that molt between basic and alternate plumages each year (for example, the breeding plumage in many passerines, waterfowl, and other families); see **plumages**.

altitudinal distribution, *n.*; see **altitudinal zonation**.

altitudinal zonation, *n.*, the distribution of species or subspecies in accordance with elevation above sea level in a particular area or region; also called **altitudinal distribution**.

altricial, *adj.*, describing a newly hatched bird with unopened eyes, scarcity of natal down, incapable of locomotion, and fed by parents; same as **nestling**; compare **nidicolous**; contrast **precocial**.

altruism, *n.*, individual behavior that appears to implicate individual risk for the benefit of the group (for example, sounding a warning as parental self-sacrifice to save its young, or attacking a hawk).

alula, *n.*, a small structure on the leading edge of a wing used to increase flight efficiency; also called a **false wing**. *See illustration, p. 148.*

alular, *adj.*, pertaining to the alula.

alular quills, *n.*, three or four short, stiff feathers near the wrist on the upper surface of the leading edge of the wing, used to increase aerodynamic efficiency at slow flight speed.

alular quill coverts, *n.*, three small feathers overlapping the bases of the alular quills.

ambulatory, *adj.*, describes a bird that is walking or running; see **gradient**; contrast with **saltatory**.

amnion, *n.*, a membrane that develops in the egg to surround the embryo and amniotic fluid; see also **allantois**, **chorion**.

anal, *adj.*, pertaining to the anus (vent).

anal circlet, *n.*, a double row of feathers surrounding the cloaca (vent).

anal region, *n.*, the feathered area immediately surrounding the anus.

analogous, *adj.*, describing a similarity of structure that is related to similarity of function in species that are not closely related (for example, wings in insects and wings in birds have some similarities in both respects); see also **homologous**, **convergent evolution**.

anatine, *adj.*, ducklike.

anatomy, *n.*, bodily structure. Also the science of systematic study of bodily structure; see **morphology**.

angle of the chin, *n.*, the point where the rami of the lower jaw come together.

angle of the mouth, *n.*, the point at the base of a bird's bill where the two mandibles come together.

anisodactyl, *adj.*, having three toes forward and one, the hallux, facing to the rear; the most common foot configuration in bird species. *See illustration, p. 62.*

anisodactylous, *adj.*, see **anisodactyl**.

ankle, *n.*, the intertarsal joint.

anosmatic, *adj.*, lacking olfactory senses (sense of smell); see also **olfaction**.

anserine, *adj.*, gooselike.

antaposematic, *adj.*, describing coloration, or the display thereof, to threaten or establish dominance.

antebrachium, *n.*, the portion of the wing between the elbow (the angle pointing to the rear) and the wrist (the angle pointing forward, the bend of the wing); also called the **forearm**.

anterior, *adj.*, describing anatomy toward the front or head.

anthine, *adj.*, pipitlike.

anting, *n.*, the practice of standing on or near an anthill and allowing ants to crawl through the plumage (stinging ants are avoided). Passive anting is practiced by some crows and thrushes, who merely allow the ants to wander through their plumage. Active anting is practiced by song sparrows, starlings, and some thrushes, who pick ants up with their bills and jab them into plumage or preen their feathers with the ants' secretions. This behavior is thought to provide beneficial insecticidal properties by using the formic acid secreted by ants, to aid in preening, or to provide relief of itching or other symptoms encountered during molting. Anting has been observed in more than 200 species worldwide; see also Terres, pp. 18-20.

apex, *n.*, the highest or most protruding tip or point (for example, the apex of a bird's bill).

aponeurosis, *n.*, a band of connective tissue, such as the patellar tendon in the knee.

aposematic, *adj.*, describing protective adaptations, usually applied to coloration. Variations include **proaposematic** coloration that warns predators, usually of unpalatability; **pseudaposematic** coloration that bluffs or mimics some type of predator or threat; and **synaposematic** coloration, which means that the warning signal is shared with other species; compare **episematic**, **sematic**.

appendicular skeleton, *n.*, collectively, those parts of the skeleton that make up the wings and legs (in other words, the appendages); contrast with **axial skeleton**.

apterium, *n.*, *pl.* **apteria**, an area of skin that is more or less bare of feathers.

Internal Anatomy
(Penguin)

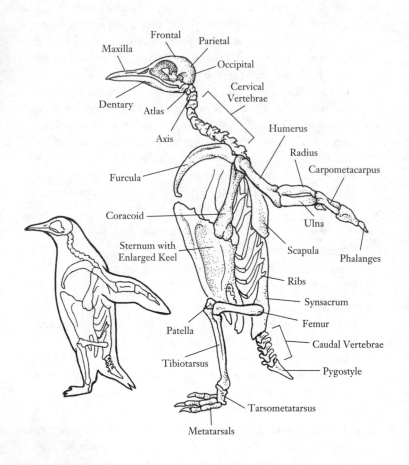

Internal Anatomy
(Blue Jay)

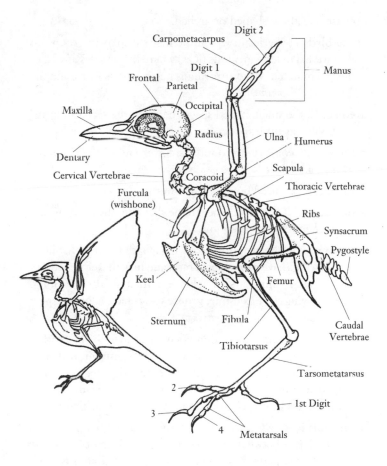

aquatic, *adj.*, pertaining to water. Aquatic birds are those that chiefly derive their subsistence from seas, lakes, or rivers.

aquiline, *adj.*, eaglelike.

arboreal, *adj.*, tree-inhabiting.

arcuate, *adj.*, bow-shaped or arched.

arena bird, *n.*, species in which the males display in groups on traditional mating grounds (leks) where the females attend to be inseminated without forming nesting pairs (for example, grouse [*Tetraoninae*]).

areolae, *n.*, the small, naked spaces between the scales of birds' feet; same as **interspaces**.

armilla, *n.*, a color ring around the lower end of the shinbone (tibia); an anklet.

articular, *n.*, a paired bone of the lower jaw.

articulation, *n.*, with reference to the skeleton, the meeting and movement of bones at a joint.

aspect ratio, *n.*, the proportion of wing length to breadth. Short, broad wings have a low aspect ratio and may therefore require more rapid wingbeats to achieve sufficient lift than long, narrow wings (for example, grouse wings have a lower aspect ratio than those of an albatross).

assortative mating, *n.*, selection as a mate of an individual within a varied population with more or less similar features, promoted by recognizing similarities in song or appearance. The extent to which this trend prevails is uncertain. Mating with a hybrid would be the opposite of such selectivity.

asymmetrical, *adj.*, without symmetry, or without close resemblance between corresponding parts or organs. (For example, the pattern of coloration in partial albinos is often asymmetrical.)

asymmetry, *n.*, a disproportion or want of close resemblance between corresponding parts or organs. Some owls show decided asymmetry of the skull, since their ears are at different heights, allowing the birds to locate prey by triangulation.

asynchronous hatching, *n.*, the hatching of eggs over a period of days, in the order in which they were laid, with incubation commenced prior to completion of the clutch. The result of such hatching in years of scarce food is that the later chicks will be less able to compete for food with the larger chicks, thus helping to assure success with the few strongest chicks at the expense of having a larger clutch; see also **automatic apportionment**, **brood reduction**.

atlas, *n.*, the first vertebra, articulating with the skull.

atrium, *n.*, *pl.* **atria**, the smaller chamber of the heart; see also **ventricle**.

atrophy, *n.*, the wasting away of an organ or part through deficient nutrition or lack of exercise.

attenuate, *adj.*, tapering or growing gradually narrower toward an extremity, but not necessarily pointed; contrast with **acuminate**.

auklet, one of several small Pacific Coast seabirds of the family *Alcidae* (for example, auks and their allies), many with crests and whiskers, which dine primarily on crustaceans.

auricular, *adj.*, describes the area below the orbit (eye area), roughly corresponding to the human cheek or jowl also known as the **ear patch**; [**field mark**].

auriculars, *n.*, feathers without barbules on the sides of a bird's head that overlie the ear openings, sometimes conspicuous; also called **ear coverts**; [**field mark**]. *See illustration, p. 137.*

autolycism, *n.*, behavior exhibiting a relationship between species of birds or animals that is based more on convenience than on any parasitic, symbiotic, or commensal relationship (for example, swallows nesting under bridges).

automatic apportionment, *n.*, a process by which food is distributed among nestlings such that the most aggressive nestlings are first satisfied, thence down to the least aggressive; see also **asynchronous hatching, brood reduction**.

autonomic nervous system, *n.*, the part of the nervous system that controls reflexes of the circulatory, respiratory, and metabolic systems, including the adrenal glands, to stimulate and regulate metabolism and "fight or flight" reflexes.

autumnal recrudescence, *n.*, reinitiation of nest building after the mating season, as hormone levels drop from mating levels to premating levels.

Aves, *n.*, the scientific name of the class of vertebrates known as birds.

avian, *adj.*, describing or relating to birds.

avifauna, *n.*, the collective bird life in a local or continental area.

axial skeleton, *n.*, the skull, vertebrae, and rib cage; contrast with **appendicular skeleton**.

axilla, *n.*, the armpit.

axillar, *adj.*, pertaining to the "armpit"; *n.*, feathers in the underside of the wing where it joins the body; **[field mark]**. *See illustration, p. 80.*

axis, *n.*, the bone beneath the atlas in the vertebral column.

Bb

back, *n.,* that part of a bird's dorsal surface described as the anterior (forward) two-thirds of the area between the nape (back of the neck) and the base of the tail; **[field mark]**.

backcross, *n.,* a cross between a hybrid (cross between two species) and one of the parent species (for example, Brewster's Warbler is a hybrid of the Blue-winged Warbler and the Golden-winged Warbler, and Lawrence's Warbler is a backcross between Brewster's Warbler and one of the parent types); see **intergradation**.

background adaptation, *n.,* the matching of a bird's plumage to the environment in which it lives; also called **background coloration**.

baldface, colloquial name for the American Coot, *Fulica americana*.

baldpate, colloquial name for the American Wigeon, *Anas americana*, a North American duck.

band, *n.,* a broad bar of color; a broad, transverse mark with regular and nearly parallel edges. A broad band encircling the body is a **zone**; a narrow color mark is a **bar**; see **belt**.

banded, *adj.,* marked with bands.

banding, *v.,* attaching markers to legs, wings, necks, or beaks of individual birds whose age, species, sex, and location are recorded both at the time of banding and at the time(s) of subsequent observation or collection. Some limit the term to mean only the placing of bands on legs.

banner-marks, *n.,* white areas on the wings, rump, or tail that appear suddenly conspicuous at the time of taking flight,

13

designed to deflect predators' attacks from vital areas; see also
deflective coloration.

bar, *n.*, a narrow, transverse mark of color; see also **band**, **belt**,
zone.

barbs, *n.*, projections from a flight feather that extend at near-
right angles from the shaft. Barbs form the vanes of the feather.

barbicels, *n.*, tiny projections from barbules that interlock to
maintain the smooth surface of the vanes to prevent air from
leaking through the feather. *See illustration p. 47.*

barbules, *n.*, projections from the barbs of a flight feather that
interlock to maintain structural function of the vanes.

basal, *adj.*, pertaining to the bare proximal portion of a feather;
see also **calamus**.

basic plumage, *n.*, the feather coat acquired following the first
postjuvenal molt. Species that molt annually have only a basic
plumage. Species that molt twice annually have a basic and
an **alternate plumage**; in those species, the alternate plumage
is the breeding or nuptial plumage, and the basic plumage is
the winter plumage; see Campbell & Lack, pp. 361-4, and
Proctor & Lynch, pp. 106-9; see **plumages**.

beak, *n.*, see **bill**.

beard, *n.*, a unique bristlelike or hairlike appendage growing
from the breasts of turkeys, usually one per bird and more
commonly observed on males. Beards can grow up to 12 inches
long and are considered a trophy by some hunters.

begging display, *n.*, a display with the head down, mouth open,
and wings up, shown by young wanting food and/or as part
of courtship behavior in some species.

belly, *n.*, the abdomen or the ventral (lower) surface between
the breast and the base of the tail; **[field mark]**.

belt, n., a broad band of color across the breast or belly. If the
belt encircles the body, it is called a **zone**; see also **band**, **bar**.

belted, *adj.*, marked with a broad band or belt of color across the lower part of the body.

bend of the wing, *n.*, the angle or prominence at the wrist joint (carpus) in a folded wing.

Bergmann's Rule, *n.*, a rule of adaptation to environment that says body size tends to be larger in colder climates and smaller in warmer climates in birds and mammals. The ratio of body volume to body surface is higher in colder climates, thereby helping to conserve heat, whereas the converse is true in environments where cooling is needed. The rule applies only within a species.

bevy, *n.*, a flock of quail or partridges.

bill, *n.*, the horny, lightweight, two-part protrusion from the face, used as a tool for feeding, nest-building, hygiene, preening, and displays, consisting of upper and lower mandibles. A bill's shape varies with the needs of particular species; same as **beak**; **[field mark]**. Bill shapes include:

> **acute**: tapering to a sharp point (for example, warblers)
> **bent**: curved bluntly (flamingos)
> **chisel-like**: straight and sturdy with beveled tip (Hairy Woodpecker)
> **compressed**: more high than wide (Belted Kingfisher)
> **conical**: cone-shaped, usually short (redpolls)
> **crossed**: tips of the mandibles cross (crossbills)
> **decurved**: curved downward (Brown Creeper)
> **depressed**: more wide than high (most ducks)
> **gibbous**: with a pronounced hump (scoters)
> **hooked**: upper mandible longer than lower (hawks)
> **lamellate**: with sievelike transverse, toothlike ridges (Snow Goose)
> **long**: notably longer than the head (Long-billed Curlew)
> **notched**: toothed (falcons and trogons)
> **recurved**: curved upward (godwit, avocet)

Bill Shapes

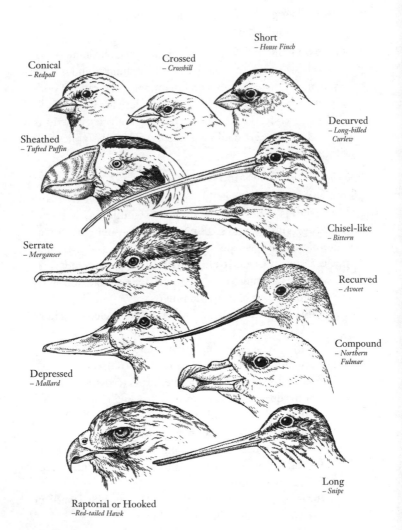

Short
– *House Finch*

Conical
– *Redpoll*

Crossed
– *Crossbill*

Decurved
– *Long-billed Curlew*

Sheathed
– *Tufted Puffin*

Chisel-like
– *Bittern*

Serrate
– *Merganser*

Recurved
– *Avocet*

Compound
– *Northern Fulmar*

Depressed
– *Mallard*

Raptorial or Hooked
– *Red-tailed Hawk*

Long
– *Snipe*

> **serrate**: with sawlike tomia (mergansers)
> **short**: notably shorter than the head (finches)
> **spatulate**: spoon shaped, widened near the tip (Northern Shoveler)
> **stout**: high and wide (grouse)
> **straight**: simple, not curved (bittern)
> **terete**: cylindrical, circular (hummingbirds)
> **toothed**: double notched in the upper mandible (falcons)

billing, *n.*, the practice of touching bills, either during courtship (for example, the House Finch, *Carpodacus mexicanus*) or when relieving incubation duties by one member of the pair (for example, Pied-billed Grebe, *Podilymbus podiceps*).

binocularity, *n.*, the quality of being able to see an object with both eyes at once. Birds of prey have a wide range of binocular vision as compared with many ground-feeding birds.

binomial, *adj.*, having two names. The **binomial system of nomenclature**, instituted in 1758 by Linnaeus and adapted by zoologists and botanists, promulgates the use of two terms for each species name. The first of the two terms refers to the genus; the second refers to the species.

biology, *n.*, the study of living beings with relation to the laws and results of their organization.

biome, *n.*, a major plant/animal ecosystem type, such as tundra, grassland, forest, etc. A biome is a higher level of ecological organization than an ecosystem; also called a **biotic community** or **life zone**.

biosphere, *n.*, the largest level of biological organization, comprising the entire habitable land, water, and air space of the planet.

biotic community, *n.*, see **biome**.

bipedal, *adj.*, two-footed, in the sense that only two limbs are used for walking.

bird, *n.*, any member of the animal class *Aves*, warm-blooded vertebrates with wings and feathers that lay eggs.

birder, *n.*, a person, often an amateur, who studies, lists, attracts, and/or observes birds, generally endowed with an incurable interest in avian behavior.

bird of prey, *n.*, any of several families of hawks and owls that are carnivorous (meat eaters); also called **raptor**.

bluebill, common name for either of two species of scaup (*Aythya*), diving ducks.

Blue List, *n.*, the National Audubon Society's list of North American birds that are exhibiting unusual (noncyclical) population declines but are not yet officially threatened or endangered.

bog hen, colloquial name for the American Bittern, *Botaurus lentiginosus*; also called **bog-trotter**.

bogsucker, colloquial name for the American Woodcock, *Scolopax minor*.

bog-trotter, see **bog hen**.

booby, substantive name for any of six species of pelagic (ocean-dwelling), diving, goose-sized, fish-eating, streamlined seabirds. Members of the family *Sulidae*, boobies are not wary of humans. Blue- and red-footed species have spectacular colored feet.

booming ground, *n.*, an area used for courtship displays by some of the grouse species, particularly the Greater Prairie-Chicken, *Tympanuchus cupido;* see **lek**, **dancing ground**.

boot, *n.*, the tarsal envelope, when smooth; see **booted**.

booted, *adj.*, describing the tarsus (leg) when the covering is smooth and not segmented. In common usage, booted is sometimes used to mean feathered, as regards poultry; compare **scutellate** (scaled) and **rough-legged** (feathered).

bordered, *adj.*, having an edge or margin of a single color.

boreal, *adj.*, northern.

braccate, *adj.*, plumelike, or having elongated feathers on the outer side of the legs (as in, for example, most members of the family *Falconidae*).

brace, *n.*, collective noun for two birds of the same species, irrespective of sex, usually in a hunter's bag.

brachial, *adj.*, pertaining to the wing.

brachium, *n.*, the proximal (nearer to body) portion of the wing between the body and the elbow, containing the humerus bone.

brachypterous, *adj.*, short-winged.

brachyurous, adj., short-tailed.

brailing, *n.*, the practice of tying the forewing of captive birds to the manus to prevent flight.

brant, substantive name for the medium-sized dark goose, *Branta bernicla*.

breast, *n.*, the area between the throat and the belly; **[field mark]**.

breastbone, *n.*, the sternum, the central bone to which flight muscles are anchored.

breeding range, *n.*, the geographical area in which a migratory species customarily breeds, usually distinguished from winter range; also called **breeding ground**.

breeding territory, *n.*, the specialized area within a breeding range that a bird will establish and defend against others of its own species. A breeding territory may include different mating areas, nesting areas, and/or feeding areas.

bristles, *n.*, feathers with a thick, tapered shaft and little or no vane (for example, rictal bristles, fringing the rictal [base of bill] region, thought to serve a tactile sensory function analogous to whiskers); see also **facial bristles**.

brood, *n.*, the number of birds hatched from a single clutch of eggs; *v.*, to incubate eggs or provide body warmth and protection for young.

brood calls, *n.*, calls given by precocial young while in the nest to communicate with parents.

brooding, *n.*, the practice by parents of covering their young in the nest from the time the first egg hatches until the young are no longer covered at any time of day or night.

brood parasitism, *n.*, the practice by one species of laying eggs in a nest of another species, common among Redheads, *Aythya americana*, Ruddy Ducks, *Oxyura jamaicensis*, and Brown-headed Cowbirds, *Molothrus ater*. Authorities recognize obligate brood parasitism, in which the parasitic species builds no nest of its own (for example, cowbirds) and incipient or facultative brood parasitism, practiced by the referenced ducks; see Campbell & Lack, pp. 67-70.

brood patch, *n.*, a patch on the belly which becomes bare of feathers and engorged with blood vessels just prior to incubation of eggs, to enable greater heat transfer from the parent to the eggs; same as **incubation patch**.

brood reduction, *n.*, reduction in the number of young in the nest, for the purpose of assuring survival of fewer stronger young, by a variety of processes; see also **asynchronous hatching**, **Cainism**, **cannibalism**, **kronism**, and **siblicide**.

brood replacement, *n.*, renesting, after nest or brood loss, by individuals or pairs that nest in regions affording adequate food and temperature conditions to allow success.

buccal, *adj.*, meaning "of the mouth" (for example, the buccal cavity is the mouth).

buffalo bird, colloquial name for the Brown-headed Cowbird, *Molothrus ater*, or the Lark Bunting, *Calamospiza melanocorys*.

bufflehead, substantive name for the small North American diving duck, *Bucephala albeola*.

bullbat, colloquial name for the Common Nighthawk, *Chordeiles minor*.

bunting, *n.*, substantive name for several of the finch species, of the subfamily *Cardinalinae*, family *Emberizidae* (including Lazuli, Indigo, and Painted Buntings), and subfamily *Emberizinae* (including Lark, Snow, and McKay's Buntings).

bursa of Fabricius, *n.*, an unpaired outpocketing of the wall of the posterior portion of the cloaca (vent), present only in young birds. Its function is unknown, but its presence is useful in determining the age of an individual. Some bird biologists feel that it has an immunological function.

buteo, common name for any member of the hawk genus *Buteo* and related genera of the subfamily *Accipitrinae*, family *Accipitridae*, all large, soaring hawks with broad wings, large bodies, and broad fan tails.

buteonid, *adj.*, describing hawks that are buteos.

butcher-bird, widespread colloquial name for shrikes, *Lanius* spp.

butterball, colloquial name for the Bufflehead, *Bucephala albeola*.

buzzard, alternate name for vulture in the New World and for buteonid hawks in the Old World.

Cc

caecum, *n.*, *pl.* **caeca**, pouches ("blind guts") branching from the intestinal tract, which aid in digestion.

Cainism, *n.*, the practice of one of two nestlings actively causing the death of its nestmate, estimated to occur in as much as 80 percent of two-young Golden Eagle nests. Derived from the biblical story of brothers Cain and Abel; see also **brood reduction**.

calamus, *n.*, the basal part of a feather shaft, mainly concealed within the epidermis, and bare (without vanes).

calcaneum, *n.*, a bony protrusion on the tarsometatarsus (lower leg bone); see **hypotarsus**.

calcareous, *adj.*, chalky in color or texture.

camp robber, colloquial name for the Gray Jay, *Perisoreus canadensis*, or Clark's Nutcracker, *Nucifraga columbiana*.

can, colloquial name for the Canvasback, *Aythya valisineria*.

canaliculated, *adj.*, channeled or furrowed.

cancellate, *adj.*, latticed; marked both longitudinally and transversely.

cannibalism, *n.*, the eating of newly hatched birds by older siblings, usually observed in owl or hawk nests where the first young hatch a week or two before others; see also **Cainism, siblicide, brood reduction**.

canthus, *n.*, the corner of the eye. The **nasal canthus** is the anterior (front) corner of the eye near the nostril; the **temporal canthus** is the posterior (rear) corner of the eye near the temple region; **[field mark]**.

cap, *n.*, a colored area covering part of the top of the head and, in some instances, part of the nape; **[field mark]**.

capital, *adj.*, pertaining to the head.

capitate, *adj.*, with an enlarged end (for example, a capitate feather).

caprimulgid, family name (*Caprimulgidae*) for any of the nighthawks and nightjars.

caprimulgiformes, from Latin meaning "a milker of goats," the order comprising the nighthawks, poor-wills, and nightjars; also known as **goatsuckers**.

carina, *n.*, the ridge on the underside of the sternum (breastbone); also called the **keel**.

carinate, *adj.*, keeled, or with a median ridge. Carinate birds are those with a keeled sternum.

carnivorous, *adj.*, flesh-eating.

carotenoids, *n.*, natural red, yellow, and orange pigments in feathers, derived from plants and probably not synthesized by birds.

carpal, *n.*, either of two squarish bones of the wrist that articulate proximally with the radius and ulna (forearm bones) and distally with the metacarpals (hand bones); *adj.*, pertaining to the carpus (wrist).

carpometacarpal joint, *n.*, the last wing joint, covered on the exterior by the alula.

carpometacarpus, *n.*, the principal fused composite bone of the manus (hand), which articulates proximally with the carpals at the wrist joint and distally with the phalanges (digits).

carpus, *n.*, the wrist, or jointed part of the wing.

caruncles, *n.*, conspicuous unfeathered, fleshy growths on birds' heads (for example, the comb of a domestic rooster, *Gallus domesticus*, or the growth on the top basal portion of the bill of a turkey, *Meleagris gallopavo*).

carunculate, *adj.*, having caruncules.

casque, *n.*, a bony growth from the top of the skull (for example, that of the cassowary, *Casuarius casuarius*).

casual, *adj.*, breeding or migrating irregularly within a range or geographic area but outside of the normal range for the species. Describing a bird observed less frequently than abundant birds but more frequently than accidental birds.

cauda, *n.*, the tail.

caudal, *adj.*, pertaining to the tail or, anatomically, in the direction of the tail.

caudal vertebrae, *n.*, the twelve rearmost vertebrae, the last six of which are unfused and freely movable, making up the pygostyle.

cephalad, *adj.*, in anatomy, toward the head.

cephalic, *adj.*, pertaining to the head.

cere, *n.*, bare, unfeathered, thick skin adjoining the forehead at the base of the upper mandible.

cerebellum, *n.*, the large area of the brain that controls muscular coordination.

cerebrum, *n.*, the large area of the brain that houses the sensory perception, instinct, and behavior functions; the forebrain.

cerophagy, *n.*, the eating of wax (for example, beeswax eating by honey guides, order *Piciformes*, suborder *Galbulae*, family *Indicatoridae*).

cervical, *adj.*, pertaining to the cervix (hind neck).

cervical vertebrae, *n.*, vertebrae located between the skull and the first thoracic vertebra connected to a rib, varying in number from thirteen to twenty-five in birds.

cervix, *n.*, the hind neck, extending from the occiput to the back, with two subdivisions: the **nape** and the scruff, which occupy the upper and lower halves of the cervix respectively.

cheek, *n.*, an arbitrary subdivision of the side of the head, usually corresponding to the malar region (feathered portion of the lower jaw).

chest, *n.*, internally, the thorax; externally, the breast.

chickadee, one of seven North American species, family *Paridae*, with black caps and bibs, white cheeks, slender tails, and perky demeanor.

chin, *n.*, the feathered area just beneath the beak and above the throat; [field mark]. *See illustration, p. v.*

chordates, *n.*, the phylum of the animal kingdom that includes the vertebrates, which, in turn, includes mammals, birds, amphibians, reptiles, and most fishes.

chorion, *n.*, one of the membranes lining the completed egg; see also **amnion, allantois.**

chyme, *n.*, partly digested food passing from the gizzard into the duodenum.

ciconine, *adj.*, storklike.

ciliary body, *n.*, the structure in the eye at the base of the iris containing muscles that focus the lens.

cilium, *n.*, an eyelash.

circadian, *adj.*, pertaining to a biological cycle of one day's length or events recurring on a daily cycle.

cirrhous, *adj.*, tufted.

class, *n.*, a group of plants or animals, ranking below a phylum and above an order; all birds, and only birds, are members of the class *Aves*.

classification, *n.*, phylogenetic separation and grouping of animals (for example, birds) into large and then progressively smaller groups, based upon probable evolutionary relationships. Classification is ranked in the following sequence: class, order, family, genus, species. The more complete breakdown includes:

class, subclass, order, (suborder), (superfamily), family, (subfamily), tribe, genus, (superspecies), subspecies; see **name**, **taxonomy**, **systematics**; see also appendices and the AOU *Check-list* for complete listings of orders and families.

clavicles, *n.*, paired breast bones described as thin, rodlike bones fused together to form the furcula, with the dorsal (upper) end articulating with the bones of the pectoral girdle. Together, they form the wishbone; see also **furcula**.

claw, *n.*, the specialized "nail" at the end of each toe, adapted for different grasping functions, including raptorial (curved sharp talons, for grasping prey or digging or scratching functions) and lobed and palmate for swimming; see **foot**. *See illustration, p. 97.*

cleidoic, *adj.*, totally enclosed (for example, birds' eggs).

cline, *n.*, a geographic variation within a species that corresponds to changes in range, climate (for example, temperature or humidity), or habitat preferences. As to birds, such variations typically pertain to color or behavior; see also **Allen's Rule**, **Bergmann's Rule**.

cloaca, *n.*, a tubular cavity common to the digestive and urogenital systems, opening posteriorly through the vent, used for excretion, laying eggs, and copulation.

clutch, *n.*, the total number of eggs laid by a bird in one nesting. Some birds lay more than one clutch per season. Or, a set of eggs laid by one female in one nesting cycle. Also, a brood of chicks.

cochlea, *n.*, the organ of the inner ear that converts vibrations to nerve impulses, used to detect different pitches.

cock, *n.*, the male of barnyard fowl, game birds, and others.

collar, *n.*, a band of color partially or completely encircling the neck; **[field mark]**.

collared, *adj.*, marked with a neck ring of a different color than surrounding parts.

colonial, *adj.*, describing bird species that nest collectively in large groups (for example, penguins, gannets).

coloration, *n.*, the colors of plumage; see also **adaptive coloration, albinism, color phase, countershading, cryptic coloration, deflective coloration, disruption, melanism, obliterative shading, phaneric coloration, protective coloration**, and **structural coloration**.

color phase, *n.*, the difference in color among individuals of the same species, usually independent of age, sex, or season (for example, **dichromatism** in the snow and blue geese, **polychromatism** in the ruff, or light and dark phases in many buteos; the different phases are sometimes referred to as the "light morph" or the "dark morph").

comb, *n.*, a bare, fleshy process on the top of the head (as in, for example, the domestic chicken).

commensal, *adj.*, describing a relationship between two types of organisms whereby one benefits without benefiting or harming the other (for example, Cattle Egrets, *Bubulcus ibis*, have a commensal relationship with cattle; the birds feed on insects associated with cattle but neither harm nor help the bovines).

commissural point, *n.*, the point at the base of a bird's bill where the two mandibles come together; also known as the **angle of the mouth**.

commissure, *n.*, the line where the upper and lower parts of the bill (mandibles) come together; see also **gape**.

community, *n.*, one or more populations coexisting in time and space; communities usually include individuals of several species of flora, fauna, or both, occurring together in a given habitat.

compressed, *adj.*, flattened horizontally; contrast with **depressed**.

congeneric, *adj.*, describing species within the same genus.

conspecific, *adj.*, describing individuals or populations within the same species.

contact calls, *n.*, bird sounds that serve to keep others advised of an individual's location, for the purpose of keeping a brood or group together.

continuous, *adj.*, without interruption.

contour feathers, *n.*, outer feathers forming the external outline of a bird, including **remiges** (wing flight feathers), **rectrices** (tail feathers), ornamental plumes, and specialized protective and display feathers.

conure, a parrot of the former genus *Conurus*, now *Aratinga*.

convergent evolution, *n.*, the evolution of similar structural features in birds that are not closely related (for example, a hooked bill and sharp grasping claws in both hawks and owls); same as **convergent adaptation**; see also **divergent evolution**, **parallel evolution, analogous, homologous**.

cooperative breeding, *n.*, care of young by more than two birds of the same species. Multiple males of the Harris' Hawk, *Parabuteo unicinctus*, assist the female with care of the young in the nest. Young from previous years help Florida Scrub Jays, *Aphelocoma coerulescens*, feed the young of the year. Gray Jays, *Perisoreus canadensis*, Groove-billed Anis, *Crotophaga sulcirostris*, and Acorn Woodpeckers, *Melanerpes formicivorus*, have all been observed participating in group defense of territories and nests and cooperative feeding efforts.

coprodeum, *n.*, the uppermost enlarged region of the cloaca, which receives waste from the intestines.

copulation, *n.*, the act of coition for fertilization. Most male avifauna, lacking a penis, copulate by contact of the lips of the cloacae. Male members of the duck family (*Anatidae*) have penes and often copulate on the water; members of the swift family (*Apodidae*) copulate on the wing.

coracoid, *n.*, a breast bone connecting the sternum with the pectoral girdle (the joint where the wing bones, the spinal column and the breast bones come together).

cordate, **cordiform**, *adj.*, heart-shaped.

coriaceous, *adj.*, of leathery texture.

cormorant, any of six species of the genus *Phalacrocorax*, family *Phalacrocoracidae*. Cormorants are large, primitive-appearing, diving, fish-eating birds. They are primarily coastal, although some dwell inland, some are pelagic, and some are migratory.

cornea, *n.*, transparent tissue covering the anterior chamber of the eye.

corneous, *adj.*, horny.

corniculate, *adj.*, furnished with a small horn.

corniplume, *n.*, a hornlike tuft of head feathers (as in, for example, the Horned Lark, *Eremophila alpestris*, or the Great Horned Owl, *Bubo virginianus*).

corpus striatum, *n.*, the tissue making up the bulk of the avian cerebrum (forebrain), responsible for control of movement.

coronate, *adj.*, crowned; referring to a head ornamented with long or otherwise distinguished feathers.

corrugate, *adj.*, wrinkled.

corvid, *n.*, any member of the crow family (*Corvidae*).

cosmopolitan, *adj.*, describing species, genera, families, or orders that are widely distributed throughout the world.

costal, *adj.*, pertaining to the ribs.

countershading, *n.*, a form of camouflage wherein the upper parts are dark and the lower parts are light, so that the bird is more likely to blend in with the background (for example, penguins). Military aircraft, especially bombers, are often countershaded; see also **obliterative shading**.

courtship, *n.*, activities involved in attracting, developing pair bonds, and breeding with mates, including singing, dancing, drumming, special flight displays, strutting, feeding, and countless other forms of behavior; see Terres, pp. 110-13.

coverts, *n.*, the smaller feathers of the wing or tail that cover the bases of the larger remiges (flight feathers) or rectrices (tail feathers); same as **tectrices**; **[field mark]**. *See illustration, p. v.*

covey, *n.*, a group of birds, usually of quail or grouse.

cranes, very large wading birds of the family *Gruidae*, order *Gruiformes*.

cranial, *adj.*, pertaining to the skull; see **cranium**.

cranium, *n.*, the bone structure enclosing the brain, comprising numerous fused and partly fused bones, including the **ethmoid**, the **frontals**, the **occipital**, the **parietals**, the sphenoid, and the squamosals. *See illustration, p. 125*

creche, *n.*, a grouping of still-dependent young from more than one set of parents within a species, during a period when the parents still come to feed their own young in the group; a sort of avian "day-care center" (occurring, for example, among penguins, ostriches, and mergansers).

creeper, any member of the genus *Certhia*, comprising drab tree-dwellers that search bark crevices for insects, often while walking upside down.

crepuscular, *adj.*, active at twilight (for example, nighthawks catching insects at dusk); compare **diurnal** and **nocturnal**.

crenate, *adj.*, having rounded teeth.

crest, *n.*, elongated feathers on the crown, usually to the posterior (rear) (as those of, for example, Steller's Jay, *Cyanocitta stelleri*); **[field mark]**. *See illustration, p. v.*

crissal, *adj.*, referring to the crissum (the zone beneath the base of the tail), often conspicuously colored in some species, sometimes used in proper names (for example, the Crissal Thrasher, *Toxostoma crissale*, named for its conspicuous red-brown crissum); **[field mark]**.

crissum, *n.*, the zone under the base of the tail, around the vent, conspicuously colored in some species, comprising the lower tail coverts; **[field mark]**. *See illustration, p. 80.*

critical temperatures, *n.*, the minimum and maximum ambient temperatures marking the outer limits of the thermoneutral zone—that is, the range of temperatures within which a particular species of bird can survive by regulating its metabolic rates, heat intake, insulation, and heat loss.

crop, *n.*, a bilobed digestive organ of pigeons, eagles, hawks, owls, and gallinaceous (grouselike) birds, used for storage of foods prior to passage into the gizzard. Also, an enlargement of the esophagus for temporary storage of food in many bird species.

crow, one of three North American species of large, black, gregarious, noisy, omnivorous, heavy-billed birds of the genus *Corvus*.

crown, *n.*, the top of the head, or the posterior (rearward) portion of the upper part of a bird's head, located behind the forehead, in front of the occiput and above the superciliary line; **[field mark]**. *See illustration, p. 137.*

crural, *adj.*, pertaining to the leg, particularly the tibiotarsus (lower leg bone below the knee).

crus, *n.*, the distal (outermost) segment of the leg, between the knee and the foot; also known as the **shank**, drumstick, or **tibia**.

cryptic, *adj.*, describing a coloration pattern serving to conceal (for example, that of the American Bittern, *Botaurus lentiginosus*).

cryptic coloration, *n.*, coloration that serves to conceal the bird by either mimicking the environment or breaking up the bird's outline (for example, the coloration of a Killdeer, *Charadrius vociferus*); see also **cryptic**, **ruptive**.

cubital, *adj.*, an archaic term describing the secondary flight feathers of the wing.

cucullate, *adj.*, hooded; having a head colored differently than surrounding plumage.

culmen, *n.*, the uppermost, central, longitudinal ridge of the upper mandible (upper portion of the bill).

cuneate, **cuneiform**, *adj.*, wedge-shaped.

curlew, one of several long-legged, extremely long-billed, brown wading birds of the genus *Numenius*, of the sandpiper family *Scolopacidae*. Many curlews are rare.

cursorial, *adj.*, adapted to running (for example, the Ostrich, *Struthio camelus*).

cygnet, *n.*, a young swan, tribe *Cygnini*.

Dd

dabblers, dabbling or surface-feeding ducks who feed by "tipping up" and reaching shallow submerged vegetation and invertebrates (for example, Mallards, *Anas platyrhynchos*, and Northern Pintails, *Anas acuta*); compare **divers**.

dancing ground, *n.*, the social display ground of the Sharp-tailed Grouse, *Tympanuchus phasianellus*; see also **lek**.

dark phase, *n.*, dark color phase of a species that exhibits two or more color phases (for example, Swainson's Hawk, *Buteo swainsoni*); see also **erythrismal**, **melanism**, and **color phase**.

darter, colloquial name for members of the family *Anhingidae*.

deciduous, *adj.*, temporary. Birds with deciduous plumages shed periodically.

declinate, *adj.*, bent downward.

decomposed, *adj.*, refers to a feather with separated barbs that do not form a continuous web.

decumbent, *adj.*, hanging down, drooping.

decurved, *adj.*, describing a bill that is curved downward at or near the tip (for example, that of curlews).

decussate, *adj.*, crossed or intersected.

deflection display, *n.*, behavior that deflects attention of predators from vulnerable members (such as incubating parents, nests, or chicks) by flashing color or feigning injury (for example, the broken-wing charade of Killdeer, *Charadrius vociferus*).

deflective coloration, *n.*, feathers that become conspicuous at the moment of taking flight, designed to startle or confuse predators or deflect attack to less vital parts, such as the rump or tail; see also **banner-marks**.

deme, *n.*, a term used by ecologists to describe a local population that is in some way different from other populations of the same species.

dentary, *n.*, one of the paired bones of the lower jaw.

dentate, *adj.*, toothed.

denticulate, *adj.*, with small teeth.

dentigerous, *adj.*, having teeth.

denudation, *n.*, nakedness.

deplumate, *adj.*, bare of feathers.

depressed, *adj.*, flattened, broader than high; contrast with **compressed**.

dermal, *adj.*, pertaining to the skin.

dermis, *n.*, the inner layer of the skin.

dertrum, *n.*, the tip or hook, if any, of the upper mandible.

desquamation, *n.*, the occurrence of peeling or scaling.

development, *n.*, the process of growth of complete organisms or organs from undifferentiated tissue; see Thomson, pp.180-91, for an elegant description of embryonic development.

devil-diver, colloquial name for grebes (*Podicipedidae*).

dewlap, *n.*, a fleshy growth on the lower head; see **wattle**, **lappet**.

diagnostic, *adj.*, distinctly characteristic or exclusively applicable; pertaining to diagnoses.

diastataxic, *adj.*, denoting wings lacking the fifth secondary remex (flight feather). The condition, found in many families and sometimes useful for identification, is termed **diastataxis**; compare **eutaxic**.

diastema, *n.*, the gap between the fourth and sixth secondary remiges noted in diastataxic birds.

dichotomous, *adj.*, paired, or occurring in pairs.

dichromatism, *n.*, a condition of plumage coloration in which different members of the same species exhibit one of two color phases (for example, Screech Owls, *Otus asio*, may be either erythristic [reddish] or gray); see **color phase, morph**.

didactyl, *adj.*, two-toed with both toes facing forward (for example, Ostrich, *Struthio camelus*).

differential migration, *n.*, migration to different wintering regions by different individuals. Larger birds generally move less far south than do smaller birds. Females of many birds of prey, larger than the males, usually winter closer to the breeding area than do the males.

digit, *n.*, a "finger" or a toe, made up of one or more phalanges.

digitigrade, *adj.*, describing the posture of standing on the toes with the heel in the air.

dimorphism, sexual, *n.*, difference in size, color, or shape between the sexes. (For example, most female hawks are larger than their mates; many males are more brightly colored than the females; and some birds even have different shapes of bills between the sexes.)

dipper, **American**, alternate name of Water Ouzel (*Cinclus mexicanus*), the only aquatic songbird, which is comfortable wading and swimming in mountain streams. The dipper builds nests of mosses and fine grasses under small cliffs and near waterfalls.

directive marks, *n.*, bright or contrasting markings inside the mouths of young birds to assist parents with feeding.

disc, *n.*, the circle of feathers around the eyes of some species (for example, owls); also called **facial disc**.

dispersal, *n.*, the scattering of young away from their original homesites.

display, *n.*, behavior to communicate with others of a species (or other species), including ritualized movements and calls such as dancing, drumming, strutting, food-begging, submitting, and other conduct designed to facilitate courtship, mating, feeding of young, territorial protection, etc.

disruption, *n.*, a form of protective coloration employing bold markings that distract from a bird's anatomical shape (as in, for example, Killdeer and Semipalmated Plover) or conceal conspicuous features such as eyes (for example, the black eye-stripe in quail, snipe, and woodcock); see also **ruptive** or **cryptic coloration**. For a fascinating, controversial, illustrated discussion, see: Thayer, Gerald H., *Concealing Coloration in the Animal Kingdom*. The MacMillan Company 1909.

distal, *adj.*, in anatomy, describing the more distant relationship of extremities to the body or point of attachment (for example, the foot is distal as distinguished from the hip, which is proximal or nearer).

distichous, *adj.*, two-rowed (for example, the webs of a feather).

distraction, *n.*, a display by a nesting parent designed to feign injury or otherwise lure potential predators away from the nest (for example, the Killdeer's broken-wing display); see also **deflection displays**.

diurnal, *adj.*, describing birds that are most active in the daytime; distinguished from **crepuscular** and **nocturnal**.

divergent evolution, *n.*, the evolution of different anatomical structures in birds that are closely related (for example, Darwin's finches, in which different species have radically different bills adapted to different feeding niches); same as **adaptive radiation**; contrast with **convergent evolution**.

divers, diving ducks (for example, Canvasbacks and scaup, *Aythya* spp.); compare **dabblers**.

diversity, *n.*, in common usage, the concept of variation in habitats in a local area; in ecology, a measure of the number of species in a community, often including some measure of their relative abundance or composition.

dominance, *n.*, social order in which one bird regularly wins aggressive encounters over another, the loser wins against a third individual, and so forth, establishing a **dominance hierarchy**. Also, a measure of the control exerted on the character and composition of an ecosystem or community by an organism.

dominance hierarchy, *n.*, the order of dominance among individuals of a species in a local group, at a feeding station, in a local habitat area, etc., in which high ranking individuals have precedence in the use of resources. **Peck hierarchies** are maintained in a variety of circumstances within a local area, whereas **peck-right hierarchies** are limited to specific locations, such as a cage or a densely populated feeding station.

dorsal, *adj.*, in anatomy, pertaining to the part of a bird nearest to or of the back, as distinguished from ventral (belly).

double-brooded, *adj.*, describing species that attempt to raise a second brood to independence after raising one brood to that stage in the same nesting season.

dove, one of several species of the family *Columbidae*, including five native North American species. Doves are fast-flying, gregarious, seed-eating birds.

down, *n.*, soft tufted feathers found close to the skin, with the longest barbs being longer than the rachis (shaft), abundant in waterfowl.

drake, *n.*, a male duck of the family *Anatidae*.

drift, *n.*, displacement of a migrant from its normal route by wind.

drumming, *n.*, sound made during mating season by the Ruffed Grouse, *Bonasa umbellus*. Woodpeckers also drum on trees during the breeding season to attract mates and/or establish territories.

duck, any of the members of the family *Anatidae*, subfamily *Anatinae*. Thirty-two North American species include eleven species of puddle ducks (dabblers), seventeen species of sea and bay ducks (divers), three species of mergansers, and the monotypic stiff-tailed duck, the Ruddy Duck. Some ornithologists also include two species of whistling-ducks, which are actually more closely related to geese; see also Terres, pp. 168-243.

dummy nest, *n.*, an incomplete or extra nest, ultimately unused but built by aggressive males of polygamous species, apparently to attract additional mates or to mark territory.

dump nest, *n.*, a nest in which unincubated eggs are laid, either by birds that are ready to lay but who lack a nest, or by parasitic birds that have not located a suitable host nest (for example, the Redhead duck, *Aythya americana*).

duodenum, *n.*, part of the small intestine between the ventriculus (gizzard) and the ileum (folded small intestine).

dura mater, *n.*, the outer of the two meninges (membranes) covering the brain and spinal cord; compare **pia mater**.

dusting, *v.*, bathing in dust instead of water, either to get rid of parasites or to aid in preening (for example, dusting by House Sparrows and wrens).

Ee

eagle, one of several large members of the family *Accipitridae*.

ear, *n.*, hearing structure that, in birds, is purely internal, with only an opening to the outside, covered by the auriculars (barbless feathers) in most birds. Owls have asymmetrical ear openings, with one higher and one lower, to aid in night location of prey.

ear coverts, *n.*, feathers without barbules on the sides of a bird's head that overlie the ear openings, sometimes conspicuous. The ear coverts, also called **auriculars**, are bounded above by the backward extension of the **supercilium** (crown), in back by the **occiput** and **nape** (neck), and below by the **malar region** (cheeks); **[field mark]**.

ear patch, *n.*, the area below the orbit (eye area), roughly corresponding to the human cheek or jowl; **[field mark]**. See **auricular**.

ear tufts, *n.*, erectile tufts of elongated feathers springing from each side of the crown or forehead, resembling the external ears of many mammals. Ear tufts are especially characteristic of owls.

eared, *adj.*, decorated with tufts of feathers that suggest protruding ears.

ecdysis, *n.*, the process of shedding feathers during molting; compare with **endysis**, the process of growing the new plumage; see also **molt**, **plumage**.

echolocation, *n.*, the process of emitting regular sounds and hearing the reflected sound waves, to aid in location of prey or obstacles during flight at night or in dark caves (used by swifts and oilbirds, for example).

eclipse plumage, *n.*, the drab plumage into which males molt prior to the molt of flight feathers following the breeding season. Rarely observed in North American species other than ducks (*Anatidae*).

ecological compatibility, *n.*, a condition under which two closely related species can live in the same area without significantly competing with each other.

ecological niche, *n.*, the "place" that a species occupies within a given ecosystem or community, related substantially to the role the species plays as it interacts with others in the community.

ecology, *n.*, the study of how flora, fauna, and other natural features interact to form natural communities. Ecology is a biological science, not a place, an object, or a goal; see Campbell & Lack, pp. 166-70.

ecosystem, *n.*, a community of plants and animals, together with those environmental features functioning as a related ecological unit; compare **biome**.

ecotone, *n.*, transition zone or "contact zone" between two types of ecosystems or biomes, with increased diversity of species, often described as exhibiting the **edge effect**.

ecotype, *n.*, a local population that has adapted to the specific conditions of a local environment.

ectoparasite, *n.*, an external parasite which, in birds, hides in the feathers and sucks blood (for example, a louse).

ectotherms, *n.*, cold-blooded creatures, dependent upon external sources of energy for body temperature control. With regard to birds, only applies to reptilian ancestors; same as **poikilotherms**.

edge, *n.*, the transition area between two habitat or community types. Inherent edges occur as a result of natural processes, while induced edges occur as a result of disturbance.

edge effect, *n.*, increased diversity of vegetation habitat in edges between two types of habitat (for example, the edge between forests and meadows or clearcuts, or between wetlands and uplands). The edge effect often creates expanded niches (feed, shelter, perching points, etc.) for birds and other fauna, but may expose individuals to higher risks of predation; see also **ecotone**.

edged, *adj.*, having a distinct edge or margin of a different color such as a leaf or feather.

egg, *n.*, a reproductive body containing an ovum, nutritive stores, and protective coverings, capable of developing into an independent individual. In birds, eggs have hard but porous shells, and are incubated at temperatures ranging from 91.4 to 98.6 degrees Fahrenheit (33 to 37 degrees Celsius) for periods ranging from fifteen days for perching birds to more than fifty days for some large raptors and pelagic birds; see Campbell & Lack, pp. 173-8, and Terres, pp. 253-60.

egg mimicry, *n.*, a form of nest parasitism wherein the parasite's eggs are colored to closely resemble those of the host (for example, the eggs of cuckoos); see also **nest parasitism**.

egg rule, *n.*, an ecological rule that says the number of eggs in a clutch tends to increase with northern latitude.

egg-tooth, *n.*, a calcareous, hard structure on the tip of the upper mandible (bill) of the embryonic chick used for pipping (cracking) the egg from the inside during the hatching process.

egret, one of several species of herons, family *Ardeidae*. Egrets have long legs, long necks, long bills, flowing plumage, and medium to large bodies, and feed on frogs, fish, and other aquatic prey.

elevated, *adj.*, referring to the hallux (hind toe) when it is inserted above the level of the anterior toes.

elongate, *adj.*, lengthened.

emarginate, *adj.*, describing a forked or irregular margin. An emarginate tail has its shortest feather in the center, so appears slightly forked. An emarginate quill has a web that is sharply narrowed where its edge is abruptly cut away.

embryo, *n.*, an unhatched bird in the first developmental phase of growth; a young bird still in the egg.

embryology, *n.*, the study of the development of embryos.

empidonax, any of several species of the flycatcher genus of the same name, often difficult to separate in the field except by calls.

endemic, *adj.*, describing a bird that is restricted to, and common in, a given region.

endocrine glands, *n.*, in birds, the ovary, testis, adrenal, pituitary, pancreas, parathyroid, thymus, bursa of Fabricius, pineal, ultimobranchial bodies, and hypothalamus of the brain, which secrete hormones to regulate bodily development and function.

endoparasite, *n.*, an internal parasite.

endotherms, *n.*, warm-blooded creatures, regulating internal temperature by maintenance of basal metabolic rates; same as **homeotherms**.

endothermy, *n.*, the regulation of body temperature by maintaining basal metabolism, warm-bloodedness; same as **homeothermism**.

endysis, *n.*, the regrowth of plumage after a molt; compare **ecdysis**; see also **molt**, **plumage**.

epidermic, *adj.*, pertaining to the epidermis (skin).

epigamic coloration, *n.*, coloration designed to attract individuals of the same species to the opposite gender during mating season.

epigamic display, *n.*, courtship display that leads to copulation. In the narrowest meaning, a display that synchronizes a mated pair for copulation.

epignathous, *adj.*, hook-billed (for example, hawks and parrots).

episematic, *adj.*, describing coloration, appearance, or behavior that aids recognition. Antepisematic implies a threat; **proepisematic** refers to social recognition; pseudepisematic involves deception. See **aposematic**, **sematic**; see also Thomson, p. 251.

epithema, *n.*, a horny growth on the bill.

epizootic, *adj.*, incidence of a disease that kills widespread populations of birds, similar to epidemics in humans.

erectile, *adj.*, capable of being raised or erected (for example, an erectile crest).

erythrismal, erythristic, *adj.*, describes reddish or red-brown plumage usually resulting from the lack of certain pigments. Certain species of owls show erythrism; see also **dichromatism, morph**.

esophagus, *n.*, distensible (flexible) tube leading from the mouth to the stomach. The lower part is often dilated to form the crop, which is used for temporary food storage; also called the **gullet**.

ethmoid, *n.*, one of several cranial bones in birds.

ethology, *n.*, the study of animal behavior, particularly of function, causation, biology, and evolution as related to behavior.

etiolated, *adj.*, whitened or bleached.

euryphagous, *adj.*, capable of tolerating a wide variety of foods; see also **monophagous, stenophagous**.

eutaxic, *adj.*, describing wings with a full complement of secondary remiges (flight feathers). Many families lack the fifth secondary remex, a condition termed **diastataxic**.

evolution, *n.*, the widely accepted hypothesis that the present diversity of organisms descended from a lesser, or different, diversity of organisms, by a gradual process of genetic mutation and adaptation to changing environmental stresses and opportunities. Also, change in the genotypic characteristics of a population through the differential reproduction of its members; see **convergent** and **divergent evolution**; see also Campbell & Lack, pp. 194-5.

excrescence, *n.*, any outgrowth, whether cutaneous (of the skin), corneous (horny), or fleshy.

excreta, *n.*, feces, droppings.

exotic, *adj.*, a species or subspecies introduced from another country or continent; foreign.

extensile, *adj.*, susceptible of being extended or lengthened.

extensor, *n.*, any muscle that extends or straightens a limb; contrast **flexor**.

eyebrow, *n.*, a line visible in the feathers over the eye; also known as the **supercilium** or **superciliary line**; [field mark].

eyelids, *n.*, the membranes surrounding the eye. Birds have an upper and a lower eyelid and an inner "third eyelid," the **nictitating membrane**, which clears, cleans, and moistens the eye.

eyeline, *n.*, a usually narrow line visible in feathers that appears to run through the eye or from the posterior corner of the eye; [field mark]. *See illustration, p. 137.*

eye ring, *n.*, a ring around the eye, of different color than adjacent plumage. Not present in all species, an eye ring can be of variable width, and is often white; [field mark].

eyestripe, *n.*, a stripe through the eye, usually as wide as or wider than the eye; [field mark].

eyrie, *n.*, the nest of a bird of prey, especially an eagle. See also **aerie**.

Ff

facial bones, *n.*, the bones that compose the skeleton of the lower and upper mandibles, including the **jugals**, **lacrimals**, lower jaw, **maxillae**, **nasals**, **palatines**, and **pterygoids**.

facial bristles, *n.*, bristle feathers, without barbules, located on the face (for example, rictal bristles in the goatsuckers, *Caprimulgidae*, or eyelash bristles in the hornbills and Ostrich, *Struthio camelus*).

facial disc, *n.*, feathers surrounding the eyes and ears of owls, functioning primarily to focus sound waves to the ears; see **disc**; [field mark].

falcate, falciform, *adj.*, shaped like a sickle or scythe.

falcon, a member of the hawk subfamily *Falconinae*, family *Falconidae*, comprising fifty-eight species worldwide of diurnal, streamlined, fast-flying, stooping birds of prey; see also Terres, pp. 269-77.

falconine, *adj.*, falcon-like.

falconry, *n.*, the practice of hunting game birds with falcons, usually peregrine, prairie, or gyrfalcons in North America. Also practiced in Europe and a favorite of royalty in Saudi Arabia.

false wing, *n.*, a small structure on the leading edge of the wing used to increase flight efficiency; same as **alula**. See also **alular**. *See illustration, p. 148.*

family, *n.*, a taxonomic classification containing one or more genera, the members of which exhibit a combination of morphological (form and structure) characteristics, and which usually have evolved from a common type; see Appendix I for an alphabetical listing of North American avian families.

fasciated, *adj.*, banded or broadly barred.

fascicle, *n.*, a bundle.

feather, *n.*, keratinous (mainly protein) outgrowths from the skin of birds, found exclusively in birds, used for insulation, flight, camouflage, attraction, and identification. The distribution of feathers is called **pterylosis**. Some feather types are as follows:

> **bristles**: ornamental shafted feathers with barbs only at the bases
> **contour feathers**: feathers that give shape and color
> **down**: feathers without shafts
> **flight feathers**: primarily wing and tail feathers used for flight control
> **semiplumes**: downy feathers with weak shafts
> **filoplumes**: ornamental shafted feathers with barbs at the tips
> *See also* Thomson, pp. 272-86, Campbell & Lack, pp. 206-10, and Terres, pp. 279-83.

feather comb, *n.*, a pectinated (toothed) structure on the middle claw in some owls, herons, poor-wills, and other birds, apparently used to comb parasites from the feathers.

feather cortex, *n.*, lightweight, spongy, rigid material within the shafts of feathers.

feather sheath, *n.*, protective tissue surrounding the germinal (developing) feather tissue.

fecal sac, *n.*, a small sac containing fecal material voided by nestlings, chiefly among the songbirds, which is disposed of away from the nest by the parents.

feet, *n.*, see **foot**.

feigning injury, *v.*, practicing injury behavior to lure predators

Feather Structure
(Flight Feather)

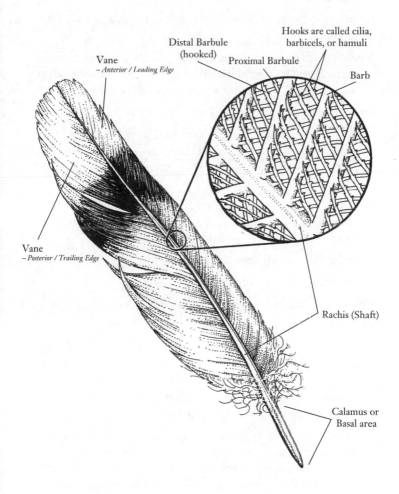

Vane
– *Anterior / Leading Edge*

Vane
– *Posterior / Trailing Edge*

Distal Barbule
(hooked)

Proximal Barbule

Hooks are called cilia,
barbicels, or hamuli

Barb

Rachis (Shaft)

Calamus or
Basal area

away from nests (practiced, for example, by the Killdeer and the Black Duck); see also **distraction**.

femoral, *adj.*, pertaining to the thigh proper (inner thigh); contrast with **tibial,** which refers to the middle leg.

femur, *n.*, a stout, cylindrical bone in the thigh; also called the thighbone.

feral, *adj.*, denoting a domesticated animal that has escaped captivity and is living in the wild. For example, the wild jungle fowl (*Gallus ferragineus*) is a feral stock of the domestic fowl.

ferruginous, *adj.*, rust-colored.

fibula, *n.*, a small, thin, poorly developed bone below the knee, running parallel to the tibiotarsus and, at the lower end, partially fused with the tibiotarsus; the thin bone of the crus (drumstick). *See illustration, p. 9.*

field mark, *n.*, a conspicuous feature of feathering, structure, posture, or coloration visible in the field, used to distinguish species and gender of birds by visual observation.

filament, *n.*, a slender, threadlike fiber.

filamentous, *adj.*, threadlike.

filiform, *adj.*, threadlike.

filoplumaceous, *adj.*, having the structure of a filoplume.

filoplume, *n.*, a slender, hairlike feather with a tufted or downy terminus (end), often found surrounding contour feathers. Filoplumes are thought to serve a sensory function, transmitting vibrations to nerves at the base of larger feathers and thus stimulating muscle action.

filtration feeding, *n.*, feeding practiced by the flamingos (*Phoenicopteridae*), which use their tongues to press mud and water against a series of stiff hairs and lamellae inside the mandibles, filtering food while spitting out the water.

finch, any of 436 species (worldwide) of generally seed-eating songbirds in the family *Fringillidae*. Also used to include members of the *Cardinalinae* subfamily of the family *Emberizidae*, *Emberizinae* subfamily of the family *Emberizidae*; all together including finches, cardinals, redpolls, longspurs, grosbeaks, buntings, bramblings, canaries, crossbills, sparrows and juncos; see also Terres, pp. 289–352.

fish cranes, colloquial name for some of the herons (*Ardeidae*).

fish ducks, colloquial name for mergansers (*Merginae*).

fish hawk, colloquial name for the Osprey, *Pandion haliaetus*.

fissipalmate, *adj.*, describing toes with incomplete webbing and lobes on each toe; same as **semipalmate**.

flammulated, *adj.*, reddish.

flanks, *n.*, the exterior surfaces of a bird along the sides, lying between the posterior (rear) part of the abdomen and the rump; **[field mark]**. *See illustration, p. v.*

fledging, *v.*, growing the first coat of feathers. When the process is complete, the bird is "fledged."

fledgling, *n.*, a young bird that has left the nest but is not yet independent of its parents.

flexor, *adj.*, identifying muscles that contract and close appendages; opposite of **extensor**.

flight feathers, *n.*, primary and secondary **remiges** (wing feathers) and stiff rectrices (tail feathers) used for propulsion and flight control.

flight muscles, *n.*, the breast muscles, pectoral and supracoracoideus, used, respectively, to raise and lower the wings.

flight pattern, *n.*, distinctive outline or silhouette shown by birds on the wing, such as raptors, ducks, cranes; **[field mark]**.

flight year, *n.*, term used for a year in which unusual numbers of northern species (for example, the Snowy Owl, *Nyctea scandiaca*), not regularly migratory, move into new wintering areas; see also **irruptions**.

flipper, *n.*, the modified wing in penguins (*Spheniscidae*).

flock, *n.*, a group of same-species or mixed birds flying, feeding, or roosting together.

flycatcher, any member of certain subfamilies of the family *Muscicapidae* (Old World flycatchers, 378 species worldwide), and the family *Tyrannidae* (western hemisphere flycatchers, 374 species). North American flycatchers have large heads, broad bills, and short legs; they perch on posts, branches, or wires while watching for insects and return to their perch after flying out to catch prey. Many are territorially aggressive; see also Terres, pp. 380-93.

flying sheep, colloquial name for the large, white Whooping Crane, *Grus americana*.

flyway, *n.*, a major migration route. With regard to ducks and other migratory waterfowl, the continental United States is broken into several zones for hunting regulation, which are called the **Atlantic**, **Mississippi**, **Central**, and **Pacific flyways**; see also Bellrose.

follicle, *n.*, the growth structure from which a feather develops.

fool hen, colloquial name for the Spruce Grouse, *Dendragapus canadensis*, or Blue Grouse, *Dendragapus obscurus*, in Montana and Wyoming, respectively.

foot, *n.*, the terminal part of the vertebrate leg upon which the individual stands, often highly specialized in birds; see also **anisodactyl**, **claw**, **didactyl**, **fissipalmate**, **heterodactyl**, **lobate**, **palmate**, **pamprodactyl**, **semipalmate**, **syndactyl**, **tridactyl**, and **zygodactyl** for descriptions of form and function. *See illustration, p.62 & 97.*

foot-stirring, *n.*, the practice by many herons and egrets of raking or stirring mud flats, shallow bottoms, and meadows to reveal or flush small prey.

foraging, *n.*, varied behavior employed in search of food. Vultures soar and watch for other vultures; finches often crowd into feeders; sparrows hop and scratch the dirt; hawks soar and kestrels hover in search of ground-dwelling prey.

forearm, *n.*, that portion of the wing between the elbow and the wrist, containing the forearm bones, the radius and ulna; also known as the **antebrachium**.

fossa, *n.*, *pl.* **fossa**, a cavity in a bone or other hard tissue with a large opening (for example, nasal fossa, large openings in the upper base of the upper mandible of a sparrow, in which the nostrils are recessed).

fossorial, *adj.*, refers to a bird that digs into the earth for habitation. The Burrowing Owl, *Athene cunicularia*, is a fossorial bird.

frate, colloquial name for Great Crested Flycatcher, *Myiarchus crinitus*.

fratricide, *n.*, killing of nestlings by siblings; see also **Cainism**, **cannibalism**.

frenum, *n.*, a mark on the head resembling a bridle.

fright-molt, *n.*, a partial molt not part of a normal molt, entailing a sudden loss of feathers, usually tail feathers or breast feathers, induced by shock or fear.

fringillid, family name for the *Fringillidae*; see also **finch**.

frogmouth, colloquial name for a member of the order *Caprimulgiformes* (for example, nighthawks).

frontal, *adj.*, pertaining to the forehead.

frontal plate, *n.*, an integumentary (horny) growth at the base of the upper mandible, as in the gallinules; also called the frontal shield; **[field mark]**.

frugivorous, *adj.*, fruit-eating.

fulmar, the Northern Fulmar, *Fulmarus glacialis*, a pelagic diving bird, one of the tubenoses.

fulvous, *adj.*, brownish yellow, like tanned leather; tawny.

furcate, *adj.*, forked.

furcula, *n.*, the wishbone formed by the two clavicles; also called the os furcatum.

fusiform, *adj.*, spindle-shaped, or tapering at each end.

Gg

gallinaceous, *adj.*, referring to members of the family *Phasianidae*, particularly the subfamily *Tetraoninae* (for example, Ruffed Grouse, *Bonasa umbellus*).

gallinule, one of several species of the rail family (*Rallidae*).

game bird, *n.*, any bird that is legal to take during an open hunting season (for example, grouse, waterfowl, dove, snipe, pheasant, woodcock, turkey).

gamosematic, *adj.*, describing appearance or behavior that helps members of a pair to locate each other; see **sematic**.

gander, *n.*, an adult male goose.

gannet, the Northern Gannet, a fish- and squid-eating, diving seabird that is the single North American member of the genus *Sula*, family *Sulidae*, related to the boobies.

gape, *n.*, the space between the opened mandibles (the opened mouth); compare to **commissure**, referring to the line where the closed mandibles meet; see also **gaping**.

gaping, *v.*, panting with the mouth wide open and the moist surfaces of the mouth and throat exposed, to shed heat. Or, breathing at a rate of 16 to 27 times the normal rate of respiration to greatly accelerate evaporation from the mouth and throat. Also, *n.*, term for behavior of altricial (blind and late-developing) young who gape to encourage feeding by attending parents; see also **gular fluttering**, **panting**, **thermoregulation**.

Gause's Rule, *n.*, an ecological rule or theory that says two species with identical ecological requirements cannot coexist in the same environment, because one will outcompete the other and supplant it.

gene pool, *n.*, the collection of genetically encoded adaptive traits of a species, population, or subgroup at a specific time; see Campbell & Lack, pp. 247-50.

genetic drift, *n.*, the accumulation of genetic variation in an isolated population, which "drifts" from the genes of the original population; see also **adaptive radiation**.

genetic isolation, *n.*, the evolution of mechanisms that inhibit interbreeding with other species, so as to preserve the gene pool of a species.

genetics, *n.*, the science of heredity, the study of genes.

genetic swamping, *v.*, overwhelming the gene pool of one species by another species that hybridizes with it.

genus, *n.*, *pl.* **genera**, a taxonomic classification including one or more species sharing a combination of taxonomic characters not shared with any other taxon (category) of the same rank. Genus is one rank above species and one rank below family or subfamily. "The evolutionist sees in the genus a group of species that have descended from a common ancestor—a phylogenetic unit. The collective members of a genus—the species—also occupy a more or less well-defined ecological niche and the genus is thus often a group of species adapted to a particular mode of life," from Terres, p. 440.

geomagnetism, *n.*, the earth's magnetic field, which is used by many migrating birds to find their way even when visual cues (landscape, bodies of water, sun, stars) are not available.

germinal spot, *n.*, the area of the yolk sac which develops into the blastula (an intermediate embryotic stage), then into the embryo.

gibbosity, *n.*, a swelling or rounded protuberance.

gibbous, *adj.*, describing a bill with a pronounced hump in the upper mandible (for example, the bills of scoters, *Melanitta*); swollen. Also spelled **gibbose**.

gizzard, *n.*, the muscular, conspicuous portion of the stomach in which food is ground up prior to passing into the small intestine.

glabrous, *adj.*, smooth.

glaucous, *adj.*, whitish blue.

Gloger's Rule, *n.*, a rule of adaptation to environment that says coloration tends to be darker in humid climates and lighter in arid climates.

glottis, *n.*, an opening in the rear of the mouth, closed during swallowing and open for vocalization.

gnathidium, *n.*, *pl.* **gnathidia**, the rhamus (branch) of the lower jaw covered by a horny sheath.

goatsuckers, a popular name given to members of the order *Caprimulgiformes*, the nighthawks and poor-wills, thought by peasants to be responsible for loss of goats' milk at night. There are seven North American species.

gobbler, colloquial name for a tom (male) turkey (*Meleagridae*).

gonads, *n.*, the primary sex organs: **testes** in males, **ovaries** in females. In birds, only the left ovary is functional in females, whereas both testes are functional in males.

gonys, *n.*, the lowermost ridge of the lower mandible (lower part of the bill) formed by the fusion of the two mandibular rami.

goose, *pl.* **geese**, substantive name for several species in the family *Anatidae*, subfamily *Anserinae*, tribe *Anserini*, which has seven North American species. Geese are large waterfowl with long necks, strong voices, and broad bills; they eat grain and aquatic vegetation.

goosander, colloquial name for mergansers, family *Anatidae*, subfamily *Anatinae*, tribe *Mergini*.

gorget, *n.*, a conspicuous, often iridescent area of chin, throat, and part of the upper breast (for example, the iridescent red or green area seen in male hummingbirds, *Trochilidae*); **[field mark]**.

gosling, *n.*, a young goose, not adult.

gradient, *adj.*, walking or running by steps; same as **ambulatory**; contrast with **saltatory**.

graduated, *adj.*, describing a tail in which the central feathers are longer than the outer feathers (as in Mourning Doves, Black-billed Magpies).

grallatorial, *adj.*, pertaining to wading.

graminivorous, *adj.*, grass-eating (for example, geese).

granivorous, *adj.*, seed-eating (for example, most finches).

granular, *adj.*, with a rough surface like sandpaper.

grebe, a member of the order *Podicipediformes*, family *Podicipedidae*, of which there are six North American species. Grebes are shallow-diving water birds with sharply pointed bills and lobed feet who carry their young on their backs and spend most of their lives on the water.

greenhead, colloquial name for the drake Mallard, *Anas platyrhynchos*, in breeding plumage.

gregarious, *adj.*, sociable, going in a flock.

grin line, *n.*, the line along the lower mandible that gives the appearance that the bird is grinning (for example, in the Trumpeter Swan, *Cygnus buccinator*; or Snow Goose, *Chen caerulescens*).

grooming, *v.*, maintaining proper feather orientation, cleanliness, waterproofing, and oiling.

group names: colloquial, not taxonomic or scientific nomenclature, for groups of certain species. Some group names are as follows:

bouquet of pheasants
building of rooks
cast of hawks
charm of finches
chattering of starlings
congregation of plovers
convocation of eagles
covey of quail, partridges
deceit of lapwings
descent of woodpeckers
dissimulation of birds
dule of doves
exaltation of larks
fall of woodcocks
flight of swallows
gaggle of geese
host of sparrows
murder of crows
murmuration of starlings
mustering of storks
ostentation of peacocks
paddling of ducks
parliament of owls
peep of chickens
pitying of turtle doves
rafter of turkeys
siege of herons
spring of teal
tidings of magpies
unkindness of ravens
walk of snipe
watch of nightingales

grouse, a member of the subfamily *Tetraoninae*, family *Phasianidae*, gallinaceous (fowllike) birds; see also Terres, pp. 449-55.

guano, *n.*, bird dung, useful as fertilizer.

gular, *adj.*, pertaining to the exterior throat beneath the chin; [**field mark**].

gular fluttering, *n.*, the process of fluttering or vibrating the gular (throat) region to enhance the rate of evaporation from the upper part of the digestive system, for cooling, without increasing the rate of air flow through the respiratory system (which would thereby increase the rate of loss of carbon dioxide from the blood and cause hypocapnic alkalosis); see also **gaping**, **panting**, **thermoregulation**.

gular sac, *n.*, the distended region of the chin, notably conspicuous in pelicans; also called the **gular pouch**.

gull, with the terns, members of the large family *Laridae*. Gulls are sturdy, aggressive, scavenging birds with webbed feet, long wings, and stout bills that frequent coasts, lakes, rivers, and dumps; see also Terres, pp. 455-72.

gullet, *n.*, the flexible tube leading from the mouth to the crop or stomach; see **esophagus**.

gynandromorphism, *n.*, a rare abnormality of plumage wherein an individual displays male plumage on one side of the midline and female plumage on the other; see also **plumages**, **abnormal**.

Hh

habitat, *n.*, the combination of environmental factors describing where a species of bird may be likely to breed, nest, display, roost, feed, rest, or otherwise occur. Often described with reference to altitude, vegetation, climate, water, and feed conditions.

habituation, *n.*, a form of learning behavior by which a bird learns to not respond to recurring stimuli that may distract from useful behavior (for example, becoming habituated to a cage or human activity and thus "tamed").

hackle, *n.*, a lance-shaped or falcon-like feather found on the necks of domestic cocks.

hackle feathers, *n.*, slender feathers on the necks of gallinaceous birds.

hag, hagdon, colloquial names for the Greater Shearwater, *Puffinus gravis*.

hairyhead, colloquial name for the Hooded Merganser, *Lophodytes cucullatus*.

hallux, *n.*, the first toe, projecting posteriorly (back), with two phalanges (bones), similar to the human big toe, articulating with an accessory metatarsal behind the metatarsus (foot bones).

hamulate, *adj.*, with a small hook.

hamulus, *n.*, *pl.* **hamuli**, a small hook or feather part; see **hooklets**, **barbicels**.

hand quills, *n.*, the primary quills; same as **primaries**.

Harderian glands, *n.*, eye glands that secrete oily solutions to protect eyes against salt water, particularly in marine birds; same as **lachrymal glands**, **tear glands**.

harlequin, common name for the Harlequin Duck, *Histrionicus histrionicus*.

harrier, substantive name for the Northern Harrier or Marsh Hawk, *Circus cyaneus*, a low-flying, streamlined, gliding, rodent-catching bird of prey. The female is brown and the male is gray.

hastate, *adj.*, arrowhead-shaped.

hatchling, *n.*, a newly hatched bird.

hawk, a member of the family *Accipitridae*, which comprises 208 species of diurnal birds of prey worldwide that have adaptations of bills, feet, and muscles well suited to predatory practices; see also Terres, pp. 476-89.

hawking, *n.*, the sport of flying trained birds of prey against living prey, usually other birds; *v.*, the hunting of insects by flycatchers, swallows, and nighthawks.

heat balance, *n.*, maintenance of safe body temperature by conservation or shedding of heat; see **gular fluttering**, **gaping**, **thermoregulation**, **panting**; see also Terres, p. 491, and Campbell & Lack, pp. 279-80.

heath hen, extinct subspecies of the Greater Prairie-Chicken, *Tympanuchus cupido*.

heel, *n.*, skeletal joint of the crus (drumstick) and tarsus (foot), which points backward and remains in the air while the bird walks on its toes; see also **digitigrade**.

hell-diver, colloquial term for loons, grebes, and buffleheads, due to their practice of diving and staying under water for long periods after shots are fired.

helmet, *n.*, a naked shield or protuberance atop the head.

hen, *n.*, a female bird. Also, a female domestic fowl.

hepatic, *adj.*, pertaining to the liver; also, liver-colored.

herbivorous, *adj.*, describing animals that eat parts of plants.

hermaphrodite, *n.*, an animal with both male and female sex organs. Rare in birds, usually occurring with one ovary and one testis.

heron, member of the family *Ardeidae*, order *Ciconiiformes*, with approximately sixty-three species worldwide, including egrets and bitterns. Herons generally feed in and nest near water, and many nest in colonies; see also Terres, pp. 495-502.

heronry, *n.*, a place where a colony of herons nests; see also **rookery**.

heterodactyl, *adj.*, feet with the second toe facing posteriorly (back) to strengthen the grip to the rear, found only in the trogons (*Trogonidae*). *See illustration, p. 62.*

heterogeneous, *adj.*, of dissimilar nature or character; opposite of **homogeneous.**

hibernal, *adj.*, pertaining to winter.

hibernation, *n.*, the act of spending the winter in a state of reduced metabolic activity, extremely rare among birds (one example is the Common Poor-will, *Phalaenoptilus nuttalli*); see also **torpidity**.

hirsute, *adj.*, hairy or shaggy (for example, the foot of a grouse).

histology, *n.*, the study of minute anatomy.

hoary, *adj.*, frosty gray or silver.

homeothermism, *n.*, regulation of internal body temperature by maintaining basal metabolic rates and using insulation such as fat, fur, or feathers; same as **endothermy**; see also **homoiothermy**.

home range, *n.*, the local area occupied by an individual during a normal day's activities, which may or may not be completely defended by the individual, depending upon the species and the season.

Toe Positions

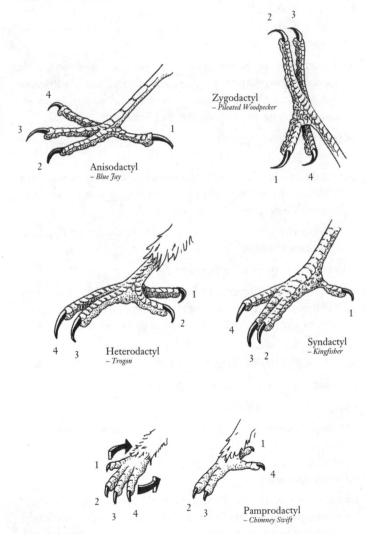

Zygodactyl
– *Pileated Woodpecker*

2   3

1   4

4

3

1

2

Anisodactyl
– *Blue Jay*

Heterodactyl
– *Trogon*

1

2

4   3

Syndactyl
– *Kingfisher*

1

4

3   2

1

2

3   4

Pamprodactyl
– *Chimney Swift*

1

4

2   3

homing, *n.*, direction-finding during migration or returning to nest sites, referring to landscape features, solar cues, starscapes, and/or geomagnetic orientation.

homogeneity, *n.*, structural similarity.

homogeneous, *adj.*, of the same character or nature; opposite of **heterogeneous**.

homoiothermy, *n.*, "warm-bloodedness," typically ranging from 100 to 106 degrees Fahrenheit (37 to 41 degrees Celsius). For most birds, this is partially developed in precocial young at hatching, and develops in altricial young about seven days after hatching; see also **homeothermism**.

homologous, *adj.*, a likeness in structural features of different organisms derived from a common evolutionary source; see **analogous**.

honker, common name for the Canada Goose, *Branta canadensis*.

hooded, *adj.*, having a head conspicuously different in color than surrounding plumage.

hooklets, *n.*, the tiniest of several types of barb structures that hold feather shape; see also **hamuli**, **barbicels**.

hooting, *v.*, calling by owls. Also, calling of birds by humans.

horn, *n.*, see **corniplume**.

humeral, *adj.*, pertaining to the humerus (upper arm).

humeral patagium, *n.*, tough, fibrous tissue that connects the shoulder of the wing to the bracheum (carpal bones of the wrist) and together with muscles, skin, and tendons forms the leading edge of the wing; see **patagium**.

humerus, *n.*, the upper wing bone near the body, a sturdy bone that articulates proximally with the shoulder girdle and distally with the radius and ulna at the elbow. The humerus contains the humeral pneumatic cavity, which receives an air sac; see **brachium**.

hummingbird

hummingbird, a member of the small, nectar-feeding bird family *Trochilidae*, comprising approximately 319 species, of which 7 nest in the far western United States; see also Terres, pp. 540-8.

hun, colloquial term for the introduced Hungarian, or Gray, Partridge, *Perdix perdix*.

hybrid, *n.*, product of cross-breeding among related species, uncommon in the wild.

hybridization, *n.*, the production of individuals from genetically unlike parents. In ornithology, the crossing (breeding) of two different species of birds; compare to **intergradation**.

hyoid, *adj.*, pertaining to the *os hyoides* (tongue bone); frequently applied to the tongue itself.

hyoid apparatus, *n.*, the bones of the tongue, including the **glossohyal** (the base of the tongue), the **basihyal** (the joint between the tongue base and the supporting bones), and the **basibranchial** and **ceratobranchial** bones (highly specialized in woodpeckers).

hyperborean, *adj.*, pertaining to the extreme north.

hyperchromatism, *n.*, the state of having highly increased brightness, intense coloration, or excess pigment.

hyperthermia, *n.*, abnormally high body temperature.

hypertrophy, *n.*, the unusual development of a part or organ.

hypocapnia, *n.*, the condition of increasing alkalinity of the blood due to an increasing rate of expiration of carbon dioxide; see also **gaping**, **panting**, **gular fluttering**.

hypocapnic alkalosis, *n.*, see **hypocapnia**.

hypognathous, *adj.*, having a longer maxilla (lower mandible) than mandible (as in, for example, skimmers, family *Laridae*, subfamily *Rhyncopinae*).

hypoptile, *n.*, also **hypoptilum**, *pl.* **hypoptila**, an afterfeather or supplemental small feather springing from near the base of a contour feather, making a "double feather," common in gallinaceous birds.

hyporachis, *n*., shaft of an afterfeather or hypoptile; see also **aftershaft**.

hyporadius, *n*., the barb of a hyporachis (aftershaft).

hyporhachis, *n*., see **hyporachis**.

hypotarsus, *n*., a protrusion on the back part of the tarsometatarsal bone in a bird's foot; also called **calcaneum**.

hypothermia, *n*., the condition of having body temperature below what is normal for the species, with related impaired functions, especially as experienced by insect-eating birds during cold or stormy weather when they become torpid or sluggish.

Ii

ibis, a long-necked, long-legged wading bird, member of the family *Threskiornithidae*, with about thirty-three species worldwide, including spoonbills, and five species in North America; see also Terres, pp. 551-4.

icterid, a member of the blackbird, oriole, and meadowlark subfamily, *Icterinae* (troupials). Icterids are medium-sized, heavy-billed birds, predominantly black, yellow, brown, and orange. Blackbirds form huge flocks for migration, and many nest in colonies. Orioles are less gregarious and spend most of their time in trees. See also Terres, pp. 936-45.

ileum, *n.*, the posterior folded part of the small intestine, indistinguishable in birds from the **jejunum**.

iliac, *adj.*, pertaining to the **flanks**.

ilium, *n.*, the largest and longest bone of the **pelvic girdle**, joined proximally with the **synsacrum** (sacral and lumbar vertebrae) and ventrally with the **ischium** and **pubis** to form the **acetabulum** (hip socket).

immaculate, *adj.*, entirely free of spots or other markings.

immature, *adj.*, a young bird, fully feathered, which has not yet acquired adult plumage but which may be capable of breeding; distinguished from **juvenile**, which is not capable of breeding.

impervious, *adj.*, describing temporarily closed nostrils in certain diving birds.

imprinting, *n.*, a form of rapid learning behavior by which a young bird identifies and bonds to parents or others to follow for feeding and care, usually exhibited in precocial species (for example, the Mallard duck, *Anas platyrhynchos*); imprinting typically occurs between thirteen and sixteen hours after hatching.

incubation, *n.*, the act of sitting on eggs. Bird parents apply body heat from their bellies or through a temporarily featherless incubation patch.

incubation patch, *n.*, a temporarily featherless area of the belly in which the blood vessels develop to increase the rate of heat transfer to eggs, usually found in females and usually not found in males. The number of patches in different species ranges from zero to three; also termed **brood patch**.

indigenous, *adj.*, native to the local area or region; see also **endemic**.

inflated, *adj.*, blown up or out.

inflexed, *adj.*, turned inward.

infraorbital, *adj.*, below the orbit (eye region); same as **suborbital.**

infundibulum, *n.*, the upper areas of the oviduct, where the ovum passes from the ovary into the oviduct; also called the **ostium**.

ingluvies, *n.*, British name for the crop, part of the alimentary canal.

inguinal, *adj.*, pertaining to the groin.

injury feigning, *n.*, a form of distraction display to lead predators away from nests or broods (done, for example, by Killdeer); see also **distraction**.

insectivorous, *adj.*, insect-eating (for example, wood warblers).

instinct, *n.*, complex inherited behavior that is neither solely genetic, learned, nor reflexive; a complex and largely unalterable tendency of an organism to make a complex and specific response to environmental or internal stimuli without involving reason or learned behavior.

insurance egg, *n.*, an extra egg laid by a species that normally successfully raises only one chick per nest cycle (for example, pelicans, some owls, and eagles), such that if one egg is infertile or damaged, at least one chick will likely hatch; if both eggs hatch, typically the dominant chick will outcompete or kill the other. The insurance eggs of Whooping Crane, *Grus americana*, are often transplanted to otherwise barren nests by humans.

integument, *n.*, the skin and related organs comprising the protective covering of the organism, including the plumage, claws, scales, and bills.

integumentary structures, *n.*, structures of the epidermis adapted for display or defense, including combs, gular sacs, spurs, wattles, and other decorations.

interference colors, *n.*, iridescent colors resulting from the breakup of light waves by feather structure instead of normal reflection of color (for example, the speculum in many ducks); see also **iridescence**.

intergradation, *n.*, cross-breeding of different subspecies within a single species; distinguished from **hybridization**. Crosses between species are called **hybrids,** for example:

> Mallard x Black Duck
> Snow Goose x Ross' Goose
> Lazuli Bunting x Indigo Bunting
> Steller's Jay x Blue Jay
> Sharp-tailed x Sage Grouse

Backcrosses exist, too, where a cross-species bird has 75 percent of one species' genes and 25 percent of another's, or an unknown amount or degree of hybridization (for example, crosses between Brewster's and Lawrence's warblers; see **backcross**).

Crosses between members of the same species but different subspecies are called **intergrades**:

Audubon's Warbler x Myrtle Warbler
Bullock's Oriole x Baltimore Oriole
Red-shafted Flicker x Yellow-shafted Flicker
Bicknell's Thrush x Gray-cheeked Thrush

The majority of intergrades are not detectable in the field or, often, in the hand. When the AOU splits a species into two or does the reverse, the "intermediate" birds can change from an intergrade to a hybrid or the reverse. (Credit for this explanation goes to Phil Wright, Ph.D.)

intermaxillary, *n.*, the principal bone of the upper jaw.

interorbital, *adj.*, between the eye sockets.

interrupted, *adj.*, discontinued or broken up.

interscapular, *adj.*, between the scapulars (back bones).

interscapulars, *n.*, the feathers of the interscapulum (back).

interspaces, n., the small, naked spaces between the scales of birds' feet; same as **areolae**.

interspecific, *adj.*, describing a relationship or interaction between two species, such as a hawk eating a sparrow or a blackbird chasing a hawk.

interstate birds, the author's colloquial name for the Horned Lark, *Eremophila alpestris*, often seen in flocks along highways.

introduced, *adj.*, describing a species found outside its natural range due to inadvertent or deliberate introduction by humans (for example, the European Starling, *Sturnus vulgaris*, brought to New York in the 1890s); see also **exotic**.

intertropical, *adj.*, between the tropics.

invaginate, *adj.*, sheathed.

invasion, *n.*, an irregular movement of a species from its normal range into a new area; sometimes used as a synonym for **irruption**.

iridescence, *n.*, a visual effect caused not by pigmentation but rather by the structure of feathers causing scattering of light rays and the appearance of metallic or other brilliant colors (for example, the feathers of hummingbirds); also called **interference colors**.

iris, *n.*, the thin muscle tissue of the eye, in front of the lens and behind the cornea, which controls the amount of light entering the eye.

irruption, *n.*, the periodic movement of numbers of birds into unusual ranges for a season (for example, Snowy Owls occasionally and irregularly irrupt in large numbers from Canada into the United States in the winter); see **flight year**, **invasion**, **vagrant**; see also Campbell & Lack, pp. 307-9.

ischium, *n.*, the vertical, thin-walled bone of the **pelvic girdle** below the **ilium**, forming part of the **acetabulum** (hip socket).

isohyet, *n.*, a line on a map marking points with equal rainfall, useful to delineate habitats.

isotherm, *n.*, a line on a map marking points that have the same temperature at a given time of year, useful to predict the advance of seasonal migration.

Jj

jackdaw, colloquial name for the Boat-tailed Grackle, *Quiscalus major*, or other members of the crow family (*Corvidae*).

jaeger, one of three species of large, gull-like, pelagic birds that steal food from gulls and terns, genus *Stercorarius*, family *Laridae*.

jay, substantive name for several species of the family *Corvidae*. There are eight North American species of these noisy, gregarious, omnivorous, colorful birds.

jejunum, *n.*, part of the small intestine; see also **ileum**.

john crow, colloquial name for the Black Vulture, *Coragyps atratus*.

joree, colloquial name for the Rufous-sided Towhee, *Pipilo erythrophthalmus*.

judas-bird, colloquial name for the Dickcissel, *Spiza americana*.

jugular, *adj.*, pertaining to the jugulum.

jugals, *n.*, facial bones.

jugulum, *n.*, the lower part of the exterior throat, lying between the gular region and the breast; [field mark].

junco, a common, medium-size member of the finch family, *Junco hyemalis*, including several races, all with white rectrices (outer tail feathers).

juvenal, *adj.*, describing the first postnatal plumage of contour feathers, often soft and fluffy in appearance, emerging after the prejuvenal molt, which occurs in different species either shortly before or shortly after the bird leaves the nest.

juvenile, *n.*, *adj.*, a young bird that has not yet reached breeding maturity; compare to **immature**.

Kk

keel, *n.*, the carina (flat surface) of the **sternum** (breastbone) to which the flight muscles attach, notably small in flightless birds.

keratin, *n.*, a hardening substance of microfibrils and a protein matrix that gives feathers strength and rigidity.

kestrel, a small North American falcon, *Falco sparverius*, also called a Sparrow Hawk. In Europe, an accipiter.

killdeer, a medium-size member of the plover family, *Charadrius vociferus*.

kingbird, one of several species of aggressive tyrant flycatchers (*Tyrannidae*).

kingfisher, one of several species of compact, sharp-billed, erect, usually brightly colored, attractive birds (*Alcedinidae*) that perch and dive for fish or aquatic insects or, in some species, terrestrial insects. There are eighty-six kingfishers worldwide; see also Terres, pp. 563-6.

kinglets, shortened name for certain small, drab, insectivorous, melodious, thin-billed songbirds, *Regulus* spp.

kite, a member of the kite subgroup of the hawk subfamily *Accipitrinae*. Kites are characterized by short, sharply hooked bills and by hovering and grasping behavior. They are found only in the southern United States.

kleptoparasitism, *n.*, the forceful taking of food by one species of bird from another, more common among the pelagic seabirds (for example, fulmars and skuas).

knee, *n.*, the femoro-tibial leg joint, concealed in most birds.

knot, shortened name for the Red Knot, *Calidris canutus*, a small shorebird.

kow-kow, colloquial name for Black-billed and Yellow-billed Cuckoos, *Coccyzus* spp.

kronism, *n.*, the practice of eating some of the young by parents, apparently to regulate population during times of food shortage; see also **brood reduction**.

Ll

lachrymal glands, *n.*, glands that secrete oils to protect the eyes from salt water; also called **Harderian glands** or **tear glands**.

lacrimals, *n.*, paired facial bones just anterior to (in front of) the orbit.

lacustrine, *adj.*, lake-inhabiting.

lamellae, *n.*, fine, almost hairlike, parallel ridges lining the bills of some water birds, including some geese and flamingos.

lamellar corpuscles, *n.*, pressure and vibration receptors at the base of feathers in the skin.

lamellate, *adj.*, describing a bill with **lamellae** (transverse and sievelike ridges) along the **tomia** (cutting edges) of the **mandibles**, which functions as a sieve or strainer for food (as in, for example, swans, Snow Geese, flamingos).

lamellirostral, *adj.*, having a lamellate bill.

laminate, *adj.*, plated or scuted.

laminiplantar, *adj.*, describing a tarsus (upper foot) that has a **scutellate** (scaled) **anterior** (front) and an undivided, smooth **posterior** surface.

lanceolate, *adj.*, lance-shaped; tapering gradually to a point at one end.

lappet, *n.*, hanging folds of skin on the head or neck, conspicuous on turkeys and some vultures; see **wattle**; [field mark].

lark, a generally dull-colored, open country bird of the family *Alaudidae*, with about seventy-five species worldwide, mostly in the Old World.

larynx, *n*., the uppermost part of the trachea (windpipe) below the glottis, not used in making calls and singing; see also **syrinx**.

lateral, *adj*., toward or on the side.

leading edge, *n*., the forward, front-facing, lifting edge of a bird's wing.

leather-back, colloquial name for the Ruddy Duck, *Oxyura jamaicensis*, so named because of its legendary imperviousness to gunshot.

leg, *n*., the tarsus.

lek, *n*., a place where males (especially grouse and similar species, *Phasianidae*, subfamily *Tetraoninae*) converge in a group to attract mates, as contrasted with performing courtship individually; see also **booming ground**, **dancing ground**.

leucism, *n*., a condition of paleness of plumage due to environmental factors instead of genetic abnormality.

levee walker, colloquial name for the Little Blue Heron, *Egretta caerulea*, for its habit of hunting crayfish along levees.

life expectancy, *n*., the number of years that an individual might be expected to survive in the wild; distinguished from **longevity**, which is the number of years that an individual might survive in protected captivity.

life list, *n*., a list of observed species, kept by birders as a personal record.

life zone, *n*., a major plant/animal ecosystem type, such as tundra, grassland, forest, etc.; same as **biome**, **biotic community**.

light phase, *n*., plumage exhibited by an individual that is the paler of two or more normal plumages observed in a species (occurring, for example, in many buteos); see also **morph**, **color phase**.

lining of the wing, *n*., the underwing feathers, especially the lesser and middle-wing coverts.

little black-breast, colloquial name for Dunlin, *Calidris alpina*, a small sandpiper.

little dukelet, colloquial name for any of the screech-owls, *Otus* spp.

little snowy, colloquial name for Snowy Egret, *Egretta thula*.

little striker, colloquial name for Least Tern, *Sterna antillarum*.

littoral, *adj.*, pertaining to the seashore.

liver, *n.*, an organ that, in birds, secretes bile to aid in digestion, stores glycogen (fast-burning fuel) for periods of intense metabolism, and otherwise aids in regulating metabolism.

lizard bird, colloquial name for Roadrunner, *Geococcyx californianus*.

loafing bar, *n.*, a sandbar or other place near water where a drake and hen can have solitude during mating season.

lobate, *adj.*, describing the membranes of each toe in the grebes, coots, phalaropes, and sun-grebes, which enables better swimming efficiency; contrast **totipalmate**, **palmate**. *See illustration, p. 97.*

lobe, *n.*, a membranous flap.

logcock, colloquial name for Ivory-billed Woodpecker (now extinct) and Pileated Woodpecker, *Dryocopus pileatus*.

loggerhead, shortened name for the Loggerhead Shrike, *Lanius ludovicianus*.

long john, colloquial name for the Great Blue Heron, *Ardea herodias*.

longevity, the number of years that an individual might survive in protected captivity; see also **life expectancy**.

longitudinal, *adj.*, running lengthwise on a body or object.

longshanks, colloquial name for the Black-necked Stilt, *Himantopus mexicanus*.

long white, colloquial name for the Great Egret, *Casmerodius albus*.

longspur, one of four species of the genus *Calcarius*, subfamily *Emberizinae*, family *Emberizidae*. Longspurs are sparrowlike, gregarious, short-tailed ground feeders; several are quite conspicuously marked.

loomery, *n.*, uncommon name for breeding colonies of guillemots, *Cepphus, spp.*

loon, family name for several fish-eating, foot-propelled, deep-diving birds of the family *Gaviidae*, with five North American species; see also Terres, pp. 593-5.

loon nurseries, *n.*; see **nurseries, loon.**

loral, *adj.*, pertaining to the lore.

lore, *n.*, the area between the eye and the upper base of the bill; **[field mark].** *See illustration, p. v.*

lungs, *n.*, paired breathing organs where blood is oxygenated, supplied by paired bronchia (tubes) that deliver air directly to thoracic and abdominal air sacs in a unidirectional flow of air through the respiratory system; see also Campbell & Lack, pp. 503-8.

Mm

macula, *n.*, a spot.

macular disk, *n.*, area of the retina in which visual acuity is sharpest.

maculate, *adj.*, spotted.

magnetic sense, *n.*, a faculty for navigation used by many species during migration; see **geomagnetism**.

magnum, *n.*, area of the oviduct in which albumen is added to the ovum.

maize thief, colloquial name for the Common Grackle, *Quiscalus quiscula*.

malar, *adj.*, pertaining to the cheekbone or side of the head, the feathered area posterior to the chin, above the gular areas, and beneath the eye and auricular area. *See illustration, p. 137.*

malar region, *n.*, the side of the lower jaw behind the horny covering of the mandible. Usually feathered, the malar region is a well-defined tract in most birds, extending backward from the base of the maxilla beneath the lores, orbits, and auriculars (eyes and ear coverts), and bounded beneath by the chin and throat; [**field mark**].

mallard, a species of large puddle duck, *Anas platyrhynchos*, family *Anatidae*.

Malpighian layer, *n.*, a layer of skin that develops into the sheath of a feather.

mandible, *n.*, either half, upper or lower, of a bird's bill. (Some say only the lower half of the bill is the mandible and the upper half is the maxilla.) The mandible is a bony modification of the skull covered with a durable horny sheath, usually hard. In some species the upper mandible is a different color from the lower mandible; **[field mark]**. *See illustration, p. 137.*

mandibular, *adj.*, pertaining to the jaw, especially the lower jaw.

mandibular ramus, *n.*, *pl.* **rami**, either of the two side-by-side parts of the lower mandible (bill). The rami are separated by soft tissue but united at the gonys (fused ridge leading to tip).

mantle, *n.*, the area including the back and the upper wings, usually of one color; **[field mark]**; *v.*, to cover subdued prey on the ground with the wings to protect it from other predators (for example, falcons mantle over freshly stunned or killed pigeons before consuming their prey).

manus, *n.*, the bony handlike structure of the wing, including the **carpometacarpus** bone and the **phalanges**, which support the skin and feather portions of the forewing. *See illustrations, pp. 8&9.*

marble-belly, colloquial name for the White-fronted Goose, *Anser albifrons*.

marbled, *adj.*, having irregular markings or blending of irregular spots, streaks, etc.

marbleheader, colloquial name for the Northern Fulmar, *Fulmarus glacialis*.

marginal coverts, *n.*, small feathers on the shoulder of the wing lying above the lesser secondary coverts.

marsh hen, colloquial name for rails, gallinules, and coots (*Rallidae*).

masked, *adj.*, describing the front of the head when conspicuously different in color from surrounding plumage.

mast, *n.*, bulky, fibrous food (for example, acorns, nuts, conifer seeds, and needles).

mating, *n.*, loosely, a term denoting courtship, territory establishment, selection of mates, copulation, or all of these.

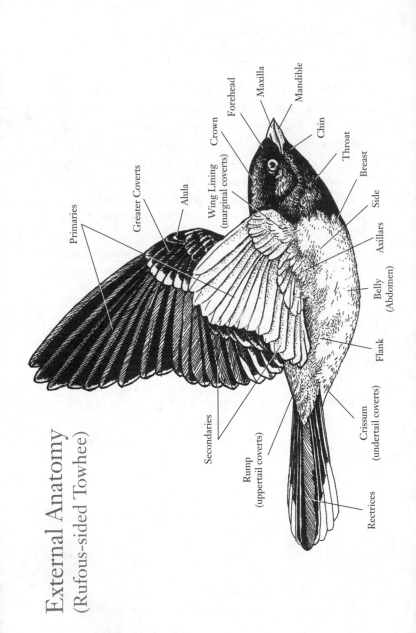

External Anatomy
(Rufous-sided Towhee)

Primaries

Greater Coverts

Alula

Wing Lining
(marginal coverts)

Crown

Forehead

Maxilla

Mandible

Chin

Throat

Breast

Side

Axillars

Belly
(Abdomen)

Flank

Secondaries

Rump
(uppertail coverts)

Crissum
(undertail coverts)

Rectrices

maxilla, *n.*, a term sometimes used to mean the upper mandible of the bill, but more properly used to mean paired facial bones that support the bill. *See illustration, p. 125.*

medial, median, *adj.*, along the middle line from head to tail.

medulla, *n.*, tissue of the adrenal gland which secretes epinephrine and norepinephrine, chemicals that control the nervous system.

medulla oblongata, *n.*, the lowermost portion of the brain, connecting to the spinal cord, responsible for reflex control of breathing and maintenance of body temperature.

megapodes, members of suborder *Galli* of the order *Galliformes*, seven genera of Australian, Indonesian, and Polynesian ground-dwelling birds, junglefowl, and brush-turkeys. Most megapodes build large mounds of vegetation in which to incubate eggs by heat of decay, sunshine, or even volcanic heat instead of parental body heat.

melanism, *n.*, an excess of dark pigments in feathers; contrast with **albinism**.

melanistic, *adj.*, exhibiting an excess of dark pigmentation, as does a bird in a dark color phase (for example, Swainson's Hawk, *Buteo swainsoni*).

melanotic, *adj.*, see **melanistic**.

membrane, *n.*, a thin, flexible integument (skin), such as the webs between the toes of ducks.

merlin, substantive name for the pigeon hawk, *Falco columbarius*, a small falcon.

mesenteries, *n.*, connective tissue holding the folds of the lower intestine in place.

mesial, *adj.*, along the midline.

mesorhinal, *adj.*, between the nostrils.

metabolism, *n.*, a bird's chemical processes; refers to respiration, heat regulation, digestion, etc.

metacarpal, *adj.*, referring to the metacarpus (hand).

metacarpus, *n.*, the three fused bones of the manus (hand) in the wing; also called the **carpometacarpus**. *See illustration, p. 148.*

metatarsal, *adj.*, referring to the metatarsus.

metatarsus, *n.*, the principal bone of the foot, comprising fused tarsals (ankle bones) articulating with the tibiotarsus, together with three metatarsals articulating with the toes; also called the **tarsometatarsus**.

migrant, *adj.*, describing birds that regularly migrate to and from nesting and wintering areas; compare **resident**.

migration, *n.*, the regular seasonal movement of birds to and from breeding regions; see also Campbell & Lack, pp. 348-53, Terres, pp. 602-8, and Thomson, pp. 465-72.

mimetic, *adj.*, imitative or given to mimicry.

mimicry, *n.*, the imitation of calls of other species (for example, the Brown Thrasher, *Toxostoma rufum*, and Northern Mockingbird, *Mimus polyglottos*, are skilled at mimicry). Or, the imitation of colors in plumage for a variety of purposes; see **protective coloration**.

mimics, mimids, members of the mockingbird family, *Mimidae*; see **mimicry**; see also Terres, pp. 610-15.

mitral valve, *n.*, the valve in the heart between the left atrium and the left ventricle.

mobbing, *n.*, the massing together of members of a species for protection or aggression, often to attack a hawk or owl.

mockingbird, the best known member of the family *Mimidae*, common throughout most of the United States. The Northern Mockingbird, *Mimus polyglottos*, has conspicuous white markings on the tail and wings and can mimic the calls and songs of almost any bird.

mollipilose, *adj.*, soft, downy.

molt, molting, *n.*, the process of shedding and renewing worn feathers to regain healthy, efficient, and suitably marked plumage. Some molts are complete (for example, the **postnatal molt**), and others are incomplete (for example, most **prenuptial molts**); see **plumages**; see also Campbell & Lack, pp. 361-4.

molting, synchronous, *n.*, a process undertaken by many water birds where all flight feathers are lost simultaneously to minimize the period in which these birds would be flightless. Molting birds typically migrate to large bodies of water during this period to avoid predation.

monogamous, *adj.*, mated with one partner, typical among birds (for example, Trumpeter Swans); see also **pangamy**, **polyganous.**

monogamy, *n.*, mating with one partner; see **monogamous.**

monomorphic, *adj.*, of essentially similar structure; opposite of **polymorphic.**

monophagous, *adj.*, birds that are restricted to a single type of food (for example, the Snail Kite, *Rostrhamus sociabilis*).

monotokous, *adj.*, describes birds that lay a single egg (for example, petrels and auks); same as **uniparous.**

monotypic, *adj.*, describing a family that has only one genus, or a genus that has only one species.

moorhen, British common name for any of the rails (*Rallidae*).

moose bird, colloquial name for the Gray Jay, *Perisoreus canadensis*.

morph, *n.*, one of the different colors of a species that exhibits more than one color or form; same as **color phase**. The Eastern Screech-Owl, *Otus asio*, has gray and red-brown morphs, showing **dichromatism**; the Ruff, *Philomachus pugnax*, a shorebird, may individually exhibit any of several colors of the species' distinctive ruff, showing **polychromatism.**

morphological, *adj.*, pertaining to morphology.

morphology, *n.*, the study of shape, structure, coloration, and anatomy, emphasized in classification of birds into groups.

Mother Carey's chickens, colloquial (nautical) term for storm-petrels, family *Hydrobatidae*.

moult, *v.*, British spelling of molt.

mountaineer, colloquial name for any of the hummingbirds (*Trochilidae*).

mountain-gem, colloquial name for any of the hummingbirds (*Trochilidae*).

moustache, *n.*, in descriptive ornithology, any conspicuous stripe on the side of the head beneath the eye, usually in the malar region. *See illustration, p. 137.*

mouth, *n.*, the opening in the anterior portion of a bird's head through which food is eaten or fed to young, comprising the bill, the tongue, and the pharynx; also known as the **buccal cavity**.

mud duck, colloquial name for the American Coot, *Fulica americana*.

mud hens, colloquial name for coots, rails, and gallinules, (*Rallidae*).

multiparous, *adj.*, producing many eggs.

murrelet, one of several small alcids, auks and their allies, of the family *Alcidae*. Murrelets are drab or black-and-white, fast-flying, crustacean-eating, coastal and pelagic birds.

musculature, *n.*, the system of muscles in an organism; see also Campbell & Lack, pp. 365-7, and Thomson, pp. 491-9.

mustache, *n.*, a conspicuous marking, usually dark, posterior to the bill and below the eye (for example, that of the Northern Flicker, *Colaptes auratus*); same as **moustache**.

mutton-bird, colloquial name for various species of petrel (*Procellariidae*).

mycosis, *n.*, disease caused by an infestation of fungus.

Nn

nail, *n.*, the horny tip of the upper mandible (bill) in ducks, geese, and swans; also the horny tip of a bird claw.

name, common, widely used name for a species, sometimes equivalent to colloquial or vernacular names, although the latter are usually restricted to a particular area or usage.

name, English, popular name for a species, which may have different meaning in different areas or countries; distinguished from the scientific names, which have standardized usage throughout the world; see also Thomson, pp. 502-5 and pp. 535-9.

name, scientific, the standard binomial (two-part) Latin name for each species, consisting of the genus name (capitalized) and the species name (not capitalized); based on evolutionary and morphological relationships.

name, substantive, the English name that is widely used for a species or several related species.

nape, *n.*, the back of the neck, lying between the occiput (back of the head) and the back; same as **nuchal**; [field mark]. *See illustration, p. v.*

narial feathers, *n.*, long feathers at the base of the maxilla (upper bill) that extend forward to partly cover the nostrils.

naris, *n.*, *pl.* **nares**, the external portion of the nostril.

nasal, *adj.*, pertaining to the nostrils.

nasal fossa, *n.*, twin depressions, visible in the exterior upper mandibles, into which the nostrils open.

nasal canthus, *n.*, the anterior front corner of the eye; see **canthus**.

nascent, *adj.*, beginning to grow, or in the process of development; emergent. A nascent species is one that is still closely connected to its ancestral stock.

natal down, *n.*, the first coat of feathers in newly hatched and nestling birds. A few species go through more than one downy coat (for example, Peregrine Falcon, *Falco peregrinus*); see also **altricial, precocial, neossoptiles**.

natation, *n.*, the act of swimming.

natatorial, *adj.*, capable of swimming, or pertaining to the act of swimming.

natural selection, *n.*, the process by which individuals of a species pass on advantageous traits to offspring. Certain traits are passed on at a rate greater than the inheritance of inferior qualities by other individuals, ultimately conferring competitive advantages on the surviving population.

navigation, *n.*, the process of following a migration route by reference to geomagnetism, position of the sun, position of stars, landmarks, and perhaps other natural factors; see also Thomson, pp. 510-14, and Bellrose, pp. 39-42.

nearctic, *adj.*, pertaining to the northern portion of the Western Hemisphere. The Nearctic Realm or Region is a primary zoogeographical division of the earth's surface, essentially coinciding with the North American continent; compare to **palearctic**.

ne-ne, common name for the Hawaiian Goose, *Branta sandvicensis*.

neontology, *n.*, the study of recent forms of life; distinguished from **paleontology**, the study of forms of life found in the fossil records.

neossology, *n.*, the study of young birds.

neossoptiles, *n.*, natal down feathers, developing prior to emergence of juvenal feathers, typically with a short rachis (shaft) or no rachis; contrast with **teleoptiles**, feathers of mature plumage.

neotropical, *adj.*, pertaining to the tropical portions of America or the Western Hemisphere; denoting migrant birds that breed in North America but winter in tropical North America, the West Indies, and South America.

nest, *n.*, in common usage, a structure built or adapted by birds for incubation of eggs and raising of young; in ornithology, a place, whether improved or not, where these activities occur.

nesting and nesting habits, for discussion of these broad topics, see Terres, pp. 627-32, and Campbell & Lack, pp. 385-94.

nesting association, *n.*, group nesting involving two or more species of birds or a bird species and a non-avian species, such as insects, lizards, or humans.

nestling, *n.*, common name for altricial young (with closed eyes at hatching), incapable of locomotion and dependent upon parents for food. Also, birds that remain in the nest for some time.

nest parasitism, *n.*, use of nests of host species by opportunistic species whereby the hosts raise the young of the parasitic species (for example, young Brown-headed Cowbirds, *Molothrus ater*). The art of nest parasitism is exemplified by cuckoos (*Cuculidae*), whose eggs are adapted to mimic the host's eggs in both size and markings, and whose incubation periods closely match the host species; see also **egg mimicry**.

nest robbing, *n.*, stealing and eating of eggs or hatchlings by birds. (For example, Blue Jays, *Cyanocitta cristata*, rob the nests of vireos, warblers, and other species.)

nictitating membrane, *n.*, an inner eyelid, usually almost transparent except in owls, used to clean and moisten the cornea. (Some researchers believe that the membrane remains over the eye during flight to protect the eye.) Aquatic diving birds have a clear, lensatic window to assist underwater vision.

nidicoles, *n.*, birds that remain in the nest for a longer time after hatching than some other species (for example, parrots, hawks, swifts, kingfishers, and owls).

nidicolous, *adj.*, describing a young bird that remains in the nest for an extended period of time after hatching and is fed by its parents; see also **altricial**, **precocial**.

nidification, *n.*, the building of a nest.

nidifugous, *adj.*, describing newly hatched birds capable of leaving the nest soon after hatching and foraging for food (for example, geese); see also **precocial**.

nighthawk, name for either of two species of the genus *Chordeiles*, crepuscular and nocturnal insect-eating birds of the goatsucker family, *Caprimulgidae*.

nightjar, name for several Old World species of the family *Caprimulgidae*.

nocturnal, *adj.*, active at night, usually in reference to feeding. Owls (*Strigiformes*) are nocturnal. Many birds migrate at night (for example, ducks [*Anatinae*]); a few conduct nesting activities at night (for example, penguins [*Spheniscidae*]); contrast with **crepuscular**, **diurnal**.

nomenclature, *n.*, names of species and larger groups of organisms. Scientific nomenclature is based upon the Linnaean binomial (genus plus species) system using Latin and Latinized terminology; see **classification**, **name**, **systematics**, **taxonomy**; see also Thomson, pp. 535-9.

nonmigratory, *adj.*, describing birds that do not migrate (for example, upland game birds, *Phasianidae*).

nonsense orientation, *n.*, description used by some researchers in the study of navigation for a tendency shown by some species to fly, upon release from captivity, always in the same direction, apparently orienting from the sun, but for no detected purpose; see also Pettingill, p. 299, and Thomson, pp. 510-13.

nostril, *n.*, opening at or near the base of the upper part of the upper mandible (bill) through which air is breathed.

nuchal, *adj.*, pertaining to the back of the neck or nape.

nun, colloquial name for the female scaup (*Aythya* spp.), after her dark plumage and white face. In Britain, colloquial name for the mannikins, *Lonchura* spp.

nuptial, *adj.*, describes breeding plumage, often colorful in males and drab or camouflage in females; see also **molt, plumage**.

nuptial plumes, *n.*, ornamental feathers acquired at the approach of the breeding season (for example, the lengthened plumes of many herons and cormorants) and molted after that season.

nurseries, loon, *n.*, places with abundant food, clear water, and relative freedom from predators, required near the nest as a condition of breeding and rearing success by the Common Loon, *Gavia immer*.

nuthatch, family name for several small, bark-foraging, insectivorous birds, family *Sittidae*, with short tails, large, dark heads, light undersides, and chisel-like bills.

Oo

oared, *adj.*, in the shape of an oar. An oared foot has a hallux (hind toe) united on one side with the anterior toes by a web or connecting membrane. The Steganopodes, including the pelicans, cormorants, etc., have feet of this character.

obligate brood parasite, *n.*, a bird that cannot attain full development independent of a host. For example, the Brown Cowbird (*Molothrus ater*) must lay its eggs in the nests of other species and rely on those foster parents to raise the young. Facultative (nonobligate) parasites may lay some eggs in the nests of other species, but are not solely dependent on the practice. For example, Redhead (*Aythya americana*).

oblique, *adj.*, slanting or running diagonally.

obliterative shading, *n.*, a form of protective coloration wherein the back is dark and gradually shades to a light hue on the belly; see also **countershading**, wherein the dividing line between dark and light is more abrupt.

oblong, *adj.*, describes something longer than it is broad.

obturator foramen, *n.*, narrow opening between the ischium (part of the pelvic bone) and the pubis in the lower pelvic girdle, through which nerves pass to muscles of the leg.

obtuse, *adj.*, blunt; opposite of **acute**.

occipital, *adj.*, pertaining to or of the back of the head or the occipital bone.

occiput, *n.*, the back part of the head, behind the crown and above the nape; **[field mark]**. *See illustration, p. 137.*

ocellate, *adj.*, having ocelli (eye spots); for example, the Peacock.

ocelli, *n.*, eyelike spots on plumage (for example, the spots on peacock tail feathers); **[field mark]**.

ocreate, *adj.*, describes a tarsus (exterior lower leg) that appears to be covered by one piece instead of separate scales; also called **booted, holothecal**; see also **scutellate, laminiplantar**.

oilbird, common name for the member of the monotypic genus *Steatornis*, family *Steatornithidae*, order *Caprimulgiformes*, otherwise known as a nightjar; also, a colloquial name for the Northern Fulmar, *Fulmarus glacialis*.

oil gland, *n.*, the only integumentary (skin) gland of known importance in birds, located at the base of the tail and secreting an oily, waxy substance for preening and oiling the feathers; also termed the **uropygial gland** or **preen gland**.

oldsquaw, substantive name for *Clangula hyemalis*, a duck; other colloquial names include **old Injun**, **old wife**.

olfaction, *n.*, the sense of smell, not thought to be important in most birds; see also **anosmatic**.

olfactory, *adj.*, pertaining to the sense of smell.

oligotokous, *adj.*, producing few eggs.

olivaceous, *adj.*, greenish brown.

omnivorous, *adj.*, describing animals that will eat both plant and animal matter.

oological, *adj.*, pertaining to the study of eggs.

oology, *n.*, the study of eggs, including their size, weight, shape, number, colors, and markings.

opaque, *adj.*, dull, without gloss; opposite of metallic or brilliant.

operculum, *n.*, a swelling of the base of the upper mandible, above or surrounding the nostril (conspicuous, for example, in pigeons); **[field mark]**.

ophthalmic, *adj.*, pertaining to the eye.

optic, *adj.*, pertaining to sight.

oral, *adj.*, pertaining to the mouth.

orbicular, *adj.*, circular, as an orbit.

orbit, *n.*, the cavity in the skull that houses the eye, and, in exterior anatomy, the circular area around the eye.

orbital, *adj.*, denoting the area immediately surrounding the eye, including the eye, the eyelids, and the eye ring (if present); **[field mark]**.

order, *n.*, a primary taxonomic category embracing one or more families that exhibit common skeletal or other anatomical features. Orders are often worldwide in distribution; see also Appendices II and III.

organ of Corti, *n.*, part of the cochlea (inner ear), essential to hearing.

ornithic, *adj.*, pertaining to birds.

ornithologist, *n.*, one who practices the scientific study of birds.

ornithology, *n.*, the scientific study of birds. Ornithology is broken into categories including **avian zoology**, **anatomy**, **physiology**, and **embryology**; **systematics**, **paleontology**, **taxonomy**, **evolution**, and **genetics**; **distribution** and **ecology**; and **ethology** and **behavior**.

ornithophilous, *adj.*, describing plants that rely upon birds for pollination.

ornithotomy, *n.*, the anatomy of birds.

oscines, members of about seventy families of songbirds of the order *Passeriformes*, most of whom sing. All oscines have four toes, three of which face forward.

oscinine, *adj.*, pertaining to the oscines; also, musical or capable of singing.

osprey, a monotypic bird of prey, *Pandion haliaetus*, which feeds on fish and is found worldwide.

osseous, *adj.*, bony.

ossified, *adj.*, having turned to bone.

osteological, *adj.*, pertaining to osteology.

osteology, *n.*, the scientific study of bones and bone structure; also, the osseous system.

ostium, *n.*, a funnel-shaped structure into which ova from the ovaries are passed into the oviduct; also termed the **infundibulum**.

ostrich, the largest bird in the modern world, *Struthio camelus*, the sole species of the *Struthionidae*. Flightless, an ostrich can weigh up to 345 pounds and stand 8 feet tall.

otolith, *n.*, a calcareous (bony) formation in the inner ear.

ouzel, or **water ouzel**, alternate name for the American dipper, *Cinclus mexicanus*; in Britain, for *Cinclus cinclus*, the European or White-throated Dipper.

ovary, *n.*, the female sexual organ in which ova (eggs) are produced.

ovenbird, substantive name for many of the species of *Furnariidae*, a large, varied family of neotropical birds. Also, the common name for *Seiurus aurocapillus*, related to the waterthrushes of the North American warbler subfamily *Parulinae*.

oviduct, *n.*, the female sexual organ in which eggs are transported from the ovary to the urodeum (a compartment of the cloaca) and in which nutrients, membranes, and the shell are deposited around the ovum.

oviparous, *adj.*, describing a bird or other vertebrate that lays eggs, as distinguished from **viviparous** vertebrates, which bear their young live.

ovipositing, *v.*, laying of eggs.

oviposition, *n.*, the act of laying eggs.

ovulation, *n.*, the discharge of eggs from the ovary to the oviduct.

ovum, *n.*, *pl.* **ova**, the female germ-cell, the egg.

owl, a member of the order *Strigiformes*, with nineteen North American species, generally nocturnal birds of prey; see also Terres, pp. 646-73.

oystercatcher, substantive name for any of several species of *Haematopodidae*, large waders with powerful bills and red legs who fly, run, and swim strongly and eat mollusks, crustaceans, and insects.

Pp

pair bond, *n.*, the relationship between pairing members of the opposite sex during courtship, mating, nesting, and raising a family. In some birds, such as grouse (*Tetraoninae*), the pair bond extends only during courtship and copulation at a lek; in others pairing extends through courtship, nest-building, copulation, and nesting, as in ducks (*Anatinae*); in others, the pair bond lasts for life, as in swans (*Anserinae*, tribe *Cygnini*).

palate, *n.*, the roof of the mouth, a structure partitioning the mouth from the nasal cavities, often forming an incomplete shelf in birds; analogous to the soft palate in mammals.

palatine, *adj.*, pertaining to the palate.

palatines, *n.*, paired bones of the skull, located between the bones forming the lower brain cavity, including the sphenoid complex and the bones and tissues forming the **mandibles**. The palatines may flex with the pterygoid and quadrate bones to allow wide opening of the mouth for swallowing of large food objects.

palearctic, *adj.*, pertaining to the northern portion of the Eastern Hemisphere; compare to nearctic.

paleontology, *n.*, the scientific study of the fossil record.

paleornithology, *n.*, the study of fossil birds.

paleospecies, *n.*, a species found in the fossil record, possibly ancestral to, but distinct from, some modern species.

paleozoology, *n.*, a branch of paleontology that studies the evolutionary origin and development of animals.

palmar, *adj.*, referring to the ventral (underneath) surface of the manus portion of the wing, or sometimes the entire wing.

palmate, *adj.*, resembling a hand. Refers to the webbed feet of ducks, for example, in which three toes are webbed; see also **totipalmate**, **lobate**, **semipalmate**. *See illustration, p. 97.*

palpebral, *adj.*, pertaining to the eyelids.

palpebrate, *adj.*, having eyelids.

paludine, palustrine, *adj.*, pertaining to a marsh or swamp.

pamprodactyl, *adj.*, feet in which the first and fourth toes can be pivoted to face front or back. Pamprodactyl feet are highly versatile and limited generally to the swifts (*Apodidae*). *See illustration, p. 62.*

pancreas, *n.*, a small, lobed digestive gland lying along the duodenum (small intestine), which secretes enzymes to digest proteins and secretes insulin into the bloodstream.

pangamy, *n.*, indiscriminate mating; see also **polygamy**, **monogamy, polygyny**.

panting, *n.*, breathing rapidly, up to twenty-seven times the normal respiratory rate, to shed heat. Excessive panting, like hyperventilation in humans, sometimes leads to increased alkalinity in the blood and a condition called **hypocapnic alkalosis,** which may cause dizziness and disorientation. Most birds that pant avoid this symptom by preventing most of the air intake from going into the lungs; see **gular fluttering, gaping, thermoregulation**.

pantropical, *adj.*, widely distributed throughout the tropical regions of the world.

papilla, *n.*, *pl.* **papillae**, a specialized developmental growth within the skin layers that stimulates and nourishes growth of a feather; a small, nipplelike elevation.

papilla proventricularis, *n.*, the ridged lining of the proventriculus (part of the stomach).

papillate, pappilose, *adj.*, having papillae.

paragnathous, *adj.*, having both mandibles of equal length, with tips that meet.

Foot Morphology

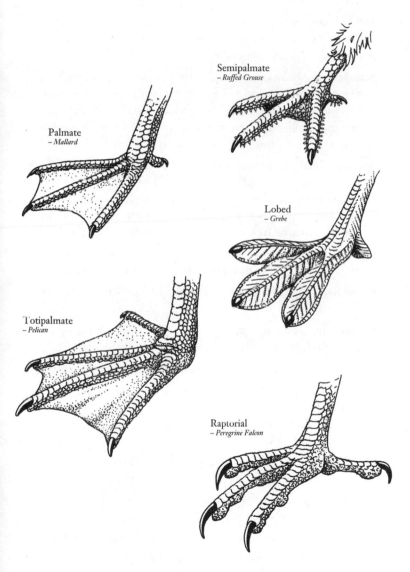

Palmate
– *Mallard*

Semipalmate
– *Ruffed Grouse*

Lobed
– *Grebe*

Totipalmate
– *Pelican*

Raptorial
– *Peregrine Falcon*

parallel evolution, *n.*, see **convergent evolution**; compare to **divergent evolution**.

parasematic, *adj.*, referring to a form of defensive behavior or markings that shift attention away from a vulnerable part of the body to a less vulnerable part; see **sematic**.

parasite, *n.*, a plant or animal that lives at the expense of a host organism, divided into groups: obligate parasites cannot attain complete development without a host; facultative parasites live independently of hosts for portions of their life cycles; temporary parasites visit hosts occasionally for food.

parasitic bird, *n.*, a species of bird that feeds or nests at the expense of other bird species. Two types include **brood parasites**, which lay eggs in the nests of others to be raised by the foster parents at the expense of the foster parents' chicks, and **kleptoparasites**, which steal food from smaller birds.

parasitism, *n.*, appropriation of the resources of one organism by another; see also **nest parasitism**, **brood parasitism**.

parietals, *n.*, paired bones of the skull forming plates above the brain cavity.

parotic, parotid, *adj.*, pertaining to the region immediately beneath the ear.

partridge, substantive name for some members of the grouse and partridge family, *Phasianidae*.

parulid, a member of the wood-warbler subfamily *Parulinae*, formerly the family *Parulidae* (for example, *Dendroica coranata*, Yellow-rumped Warbler).

passage migrant, or **bird of passage**, *n.*, a migrant observed in an area between summer and winter habitats.

passenger pigeon, *Ectopistes migratorius*, an extinct North American member of the family *Columbidae*.

passeres, *n.*, a group of birds including the thrushes, warblers, sparrows, and crows; among the most highly developed orders.

passerine, *adj.*, pertaining to the passeres.

passerines, birds belonging to the land-dwelling order *Passeriformes*, often called perching birds or songbirds. All passerines have four toes (not webbed), with one, the hallux, facing back, and eutaxic wings.

patagium, patagia, *n.*, a fold of skin in a wing running from the upper arm to the forearm. The **humeral patagium** is a smaller, somewhat triangular fold of skin running from the posterior of the brachium to the trunk. *See illustration, p. 148.*

patella, *n.*, a small bone in the front of the knee joint, not present in all birds.

patristic, *adj.*, taxonomic term describing features that are similar due to common ancestry; distinguished from resemblances due to **convergent evolution**; see also **homologous**.

peck hierarchy, *n.*, see **dominance hierarchy**.

peck-order, *n.*, dominance heirarchy established by pecking between dominant and subordinate birds in a local group.

peck-right system, *n.*, dominance relationships among confined domestic fowl or at feeding stations, sometimes involving complex arrangements where A dominates B, B dominates C, and C dominates A.

pecten, *n.*, a comblike structure in the eye that furnishes nutrients and oxygen to the inner eye, among other functions.

pectinated, *adj.*, describes a serrated (comblike) edge of the claw on the middle toe of some species and on the sides of the toes in some of the grouse (*Tetraoninae*), used for grooming feathers.

pectination, *n.*, a comblike toothing.

pectoral, *adj.*, pertaining to the breast.

pectoral girdle, *n.*, the shoulder girdle, where the wing bones (humerus), and thoracic bones (scapula, coracoid, and clavicle) articulate with the spinal column.

pectus, *n.*, the breast.

peep, *n.*, general name for small shorebirds that are difficult to identify, especially in winter plumage.

pelagic, *adj.*, of, relating to, or living in the open ocean (for example, albatross [*Diomedeidae*]).

pelican, one of two species of the family *Pelecanidae*, coastal- or inland-dwelling, fish-eating, large water birds famed for graceful soaring and gliding.

pellet, *n.*, regurgitated mass of undigestible matter, such as fur, bones, and feathers.

pelvic girdle, *n.*, the structural bone system at the base of the spinal column providing support for the legs, consisting of three fused bones (the ilium, the ischium, and the pubis), closely attached and fused to the vertebral column.

pen, *n.*, name for a female swan (*Cygnini*).

penna, *n.*, *pl.*, **pennae**, a contour feather, as distinguished from **down** and **filoplumes**.

penis, *n.*, male sex organ, undeveloped in most birds except ducks.

pennaceous, *adj.*, describes feather vanes that are firm and bladelike and distal from the basal area, which is bare of vanes.

perching birds, common phrase for the passerines, order *Passeriformes*.

perforate, *adj.*, pierced through. Often refers to nostrils that connect due to the absence of a septum, as in American vultures (*Cathartidae*); same as **pervious**.

pericardium, *n.*, the membrane surrounding the heart.

periotic capsule, *n.*, a bulbous structure of the skull enclosing the inner ear.

peritoneum, *n.*, the membrane lining the abdominal cavity.

pervious, *adj.*, open; see **perforate**.

pessulus, *n.*, a bony structure within the syrinx used to produce sound.

phalanx, *n.*, *pl.* **phalanges**, digit bones (finger bones in the wing, toe bones in the feet). Most birds have three or four toe digits, two wing digits, and some digits contain only one phalanx.

phalarope, family and substantive name for colorful, small shorebirds in which the females, brightly marked, initiate mating (*Phalaropodidae*).

phaneric coloration, *n.*, coloration that promotes the conspicuousness of a bird to provide breeding attraction, invite group feeding, advertise danger, or give territorial warnings; opposite of **cryptic coloration**.

pharynx, *n.*, the cavity of the throat behind the mouth, leading to the esophagus and the glottis.

phase, *n.*, a variation of coloration within a species irrespective of age, gender, or season (for example, hawks in dark or light phases); same as **morph**.

phasianid, family name for the pheasants (*Phasianidae*).

pheasant, substantive name for numerous species of *Phasianidae* and commonly used in the United States and Britain for the Ring-necked Pheasant, *Phasianus colchicus*; see also Terres, pp. 687-727.

phenetic, *adj.*, taxonomic grouping based upon similarities that may or may not also be evidence of a phylogenetic (evolutionary) relationship.

philopatry, *n.*, tendency to return to the same nest site year after year; also termed **site tenacity**, **site fidelity**.

phoebe, substantive name for one of several medium-sized flycatchers, family *Tyrannidae*, with long tails, slender bills, and a preference for nesting near farmhouses and bridges.

phyletic, *adj.*, equivalent to **phylogenetic**.

phylogenetic, *adj.*, derived from **phylogeny**, describing a relationship based upon a common evolutionary history.

phylogeny, *n.*, a system for classifying organisms into groups, ranking from the most primitive to the most advanced in accord with evolutionary history. Also, the history of evolutionary development of a genetically related group of organisms.

phylum, *n.*, one of the primary divisions of the animal kingdom (for example, the phylum *Chordata*, which in turn is divided into subphyla, such as *Vertebrata*, which in turn is divided into classes, such as *Aves*).

physiognomy, *n.*, a general appearance or countenance.

physiology, *n.*, the study of the function and relationships of body organs, including metabolism, respiration, circulation, digestion, fertilization, sensory perception, reproductive function, and more.

pia mater, *n.*, the inner membrane that covers the spinal nerves and brain; see also **dura mater**.

picid, family name for the woodpeckers (*Picidae*).

picine, *adj.*, woodpecker-like.

picket-tail, colloquial name for the Northern Pintail duck, *Anas acuta*.

pigeon, one of several species of the family *Columbidae*, order *Columbiformes*. Pigeons are swift-flying, seed-eating, small-headed birds that frequently congregate in large flocks, but are usually larger than the closely related doves.

pileated, *adj.*, crested (for example, the Pileated Woodpecker, *Dryocopus pileatus*).

pileum, *n.*, the whole top of the head from the forehead to the nape, including the forehead, vertex (crown), and occiput.

pill-will, colloquial name for the Willet, *Catoptrophorus semipalmatus*, a sandpiper.

pinfeather, *n.*, an incompletely developed feather still encased in its horny growth sheath.

pinion, *n.*, the distal (outer) part of the wing, including the primary flight feathers and the bones of the manus (hand); often removed from captive yard birds to prevent their escape.

pinioning, *v.*, removing one wing at the carpal joint, thus removing the manus and the primary flight feathers, for the purpose of keeping captive birds from escaping.

pink-eyed diver, colloquial name for the Horned Grebe, *Podiceps auritus*.

pinnate, *adj.*, having winglike tufts of elongated feathers on the neck.

pinniform, *adj.*, finlike (for example, a penguin's wing).

pintail, shortened name for the Northern Pintail duck, *Anas acuta*.

pioneering, *adj.*, a term applied to a species that will readily move into new areas to nest (for example, Spotted Sandpiper, *Actitis macularia*, which, unlike most sandpipers, breeds in temperate areas instead of the Arctic and will continue to colonize new sites despite lack of nest success).

pipit, family name for pipits and wagtails, family *Motacillidae*. Pipits are arctic and mountain-breeding, slender insect-eaters that wag their tails while walking.

pipping, *v.*, cracking the egg from the inside in the hatching process.

piracy, *n.*, theft of food by one bird from another, often inter-species behavior.

piscivorous, *adj.*, feeding upon fish.

planta, *n.*, the rear face of the tarsus (lower leg).

plantar, *adj.*, pertaining to the posterior (back) surface of the tarsus (lower leg).

plantigrade, *adj.*, walking on the back of the tarsus.

pleural cavities, *n.*, paired subdivisions of the thoracic cavity, holding the lungs and air sacs.

plover, family and substantive name for short-necked, usually short-billed migratory shorebirds of the family *Charadriidae*. Most plovers are smaller than most sandpipers (*Scolopacidae*); see also Terres, pp. 740-6.

plumaceous, *adj.*, describing the soft and downy basal portion of many feathers, the proximal part.

plumage, *n.*, the feather covering of a bird. Also, a particular phase of appearance in a bird's life (for example, juvenal plumage, nuptial [breeding] plumage); also termed **ptilosis**.

plumages, *n.*, the feathering and appearance of birds during various stages of maturity and later, seasonally. Most passerine birds and waterfowl molt twice a year. In order of appearance, their plumages are:

Traditional description: **natal down, juvenal, first winter, first nuptial** (breeding), **second winter, second nuptial** (fully mature breeding in many species), **third winter**, etc.

Modern description: **natal,** **juvenal, first basic, first alternate** (breeding), **second basic, second alternate** (fully adult breeding in many species), etc.

plumages, abnormal, *n.*; see **albescence** (albinism combined with looseness and poor interlocking of feathers, giving a hairy look); **albinism** (partial or complete loss of pigmentation); **erythristic** (reddish coloration in several polymorphic species); **gynandromorphism** (a rare condition of appearing female on one side and male on the other side of the midline); **leucism** (paleness due to factors other than genetics); **melanism** (excess of dark pigments); **xanthochroism** (excess yellow pigments).

plume, *n.*, a long or otherwise conspicuous feather distinctive from its surrounding feathers, used for displays (for example, a peacock tail feather).

plumiped, *adj.*, having feathered feet.

plumose, *adj.*, feathered.

plumula, *n.*, a down feather in a mature bird; natal down feathers are **neossoptiles**.

plumulaceous, *adj.*, downy.

poacher, colloquial name for American Wigeon, *Anas americana*, for its habit of feeding on parts of water plants uprooted by Canvasbacks, swans, and scaups.

pochard, substantive name for several species of diving ducks, including five North American species of the genus *Aythya*.

pocket-bird, a colloquial name for the Scarlet Tanager, *Pirangea olivacea*.

podotheca, *n.*, the horny covering of the nonfeathered parts of legs and feet.

pogonium, *n.*, the web of a feather.

poikilotherms, *n.*, animals that must use environmental energy and behavioral adaptations to regulate their body temperature, often called "cold-blooded" (for example, reptiles); also called **ectotherms**.

poke, colloquial name for several of the herons and bitterns (*Ardeidae*).

politician, colloquial name for the White-eyed Vireo, *Vireo griseus*, for its habit of placing bits of newspaper in its nest.

pollex, *n.*, the first digit (or "thumb") of the manus (hand), which supports and controls movement of the alula for flight control; see also **wing**.

polyandry, *n.*, behavior practiced by a female mating with multiple mates during the same breeding season. Polyandry is rare among birds. It is less rare to observe more than one male attending a nest (as do, for example, Spotted Sandpiper males, *Actitis macularia*). In the practice of sequential polyandry (a female having more than one mate), the female mates, lays the eggs, leaves the male to incubate, and moves to a new nest to repeat the process (as do, for example, Spotted Sandpipers, *Actitis macularia*; Red-necked Phalaropes, *Phalaropus lobatus*; and Red Phalaropes, *Phalaropus fulicaria*). In the practice of simultaneous polyandry, the female maintains a large territory in which males simultaneously incubate eggs and care for the young (as do Northern Jacanas, *Jacana spinosa*). See also **polygamous**, **polygyny**, **promiscuity**.

polychromatism, *n.*, a condition of plumage coloration in which different members of the same species exhibit one of several (more than two) color phases (for example Swainson's Hawks, *Buteo swainsoni*, which may be light, dark [melanistic], or intergraded between these extremes).

polygamous, *adj.*, having more than one mate at a time by either gender; see **polygyny**, **promiscuity**, **polyandry**.

polygamy, *n.*, the practice of having more than one mate; see also **pangamy**, **promiscuity**.

polygyny, *n.*, a male mating with multiple females during the same breeding season. Hummingbirds (*Trochilidae*) and grouse (*Tetraoninae*) are polygynous; see **polyandry**, **polygamous**, **promiscuity**; see also Thomson, pp. 655-8.

polymorphism, *n.*, coexistence in a single interbreeding population of two (dimorphism) or more genetically determined distinct color phases; see also **polychromatism**.

polytokous, *adj.*, producing many eggs or young; same as **multiparous**.

polytypic, *adj.*, a taxon (classification unit) with more than one member. (For example, a polytypic genus contains more than one species; a polytypic order contains more than one family.)

pond guinea, colloquial name for the American Bittern, *Botaurus lentiginosus*.

pond hen, colloquial name for coots and gallinules (*Rallidae*).

pond sheldrake, colloquial name for the Common Merganser, *Mergus merganser*.

poor-will, substantive name for *Phalaenoptilus nuttallii*, member of the nightjar, whip-poor-will, nighthawk family *Caprimulgidae*.

pope, colloquial name for the Painted Bunting, *Passerina ciris*.

population, *n.*, a group of individuals of a species coexisting in the same time and space. Usually, members of a population interbreed freely with each other and less freely with members of other populations.

posterior, *adj.*, toward the rear; opposite of **anterior**.

postjuvenal, *adj.*, describes the molt from juvenal plumage to the first winter plumage in late summer or fall of the bird's first year, which may or may not be a complete replacement of the plumage.

postnatal, *adj.*, referring to the first "real" plumage of a young bird; see **prejuvenal**.

postnuptial, *adj.*, describes the molt from the nuptial (breeding) plumage to the winter plumage immediately after the nesting season, which is usually complete; see also **molt**.

postocular, postorbital, *adj.*, in back of the eye.

powder-down feathers, *n.*, specialized feathers that shed keratin cells to dust other feathers with a water-resistant powder. Their appearance is similar to normal down feathers.

preacher, colloquial name for the Wood Stork, *Mycteria americana*, or the Ovenbird, *Seiurus aurocapillus*.

precocial, or **precocious**, *adj.*, describing a newly hatched bird with opened eyes, extensive down, and capability of locomotion; see also **altricial** and **nidicolous**.

precocious flight, *n.*, flying by young birds before they reach full size. Some of the megapodes fly shortly after hatching; young grouse and partridges grow a miniature set of flight feathers.

preen gland, *n.*, see **oil gland**, **uropygial gland**.

preening, *n.*, the process of drawing individual feathers through the bill to remove dirt and parasites, straighten the barbs, and spread oil from the oil gland throughout the feathers; see also **allopreening**.

preening invitation, *n.*, unusual practice by some species of bowing head and ruffling feathers to invite the other to preen it, observed in Brown-headed and Bronzed Cowbirds (*Molothrus spp.*).

prejuvenal, *adj.*, describes the first complete molt of a bird's plumage, from natal down to juvenal plumage; also known as **postnatal molt**; see also **molt**.

prenuptial, *adj.*, describes the molt from the winter plumage to the nuptial (breeding) plumage; see also **molt**.

primaries, *n.*, the largest and outermost remiges (flight feathers) of the wing, usually ten, numbered from the inside out, attached to the manus; **[field mark]**. *See illustration, p. 148.*

proaposematic, *adj.*, describing markings that warn predators, usually of unpalatability.

proepisematic, *adj.*, describing markings that serve to ensure recognition or promote maintenance of contact of family or feeding groups, such as white nuchal (nape) markings in nestling shorebirds; see also **sematic, episematic**.

promiscuity, *n.*, the act of having more than one mate; see **polygamy, polygyny**, and **polyandry**.

pronating, *v.*, rotating the wing's leading edge downward for increased lift; opposite of **supinating**.

proprioception, *n.*, the brain's sense of where the limbs are and what they are doing.

protective coloration, *n.*, a defensive mechanism by which feathers are marked to either blend in with the habitat or disrupt the outlines of a bird; also called mimicry; see also **obliterative shading**, **countershading**, **ruptive**, **disruption**.

proventriculus, *n.*, the glandular stomach of birds that stores and partly digests food before it enters the gizzard, located between the crop and the gizzard in those birds with a crop.

proximal, *adj.*, in anatomy, nearer to the center of the body or the point of attachment of a limb; opposite of **distal**.

pseudaposematic, *adj.*, describing coloration that bluffs or mimics some type of predator or threat.

psilopaedic, *adj.*, describing young that are either naked at hatching or have only sparse down on the dorsal region (back); distinguished from **ptilopaedic**; see also **altricial**.

ptarmigan, one of three North American species of the genus *Lagopus*, family *Phasianidae*. Ptarmigan are partridgelike birds found in harsh mountainous or arctic environs, white in winter and brown and white in summer.

pterosaurs, *n.*, prehistoric flying reptiles thought not to be related to birds; see also **thecodonts**.

pterygoids, *n.*, paired bones of the skull connecting the palatines, which support the lower mandible (maxilla), to the quadrates at the sides of the lower brain cavity.

pteryla, *n.*, *pl.* **pterylae**, feather tract, or a feathered area of skin.

pterylography, *n.*, the study of the patterns of growth and distribution of feathers (pterylae) on the body, equivalent to "mapping" the feathers.

pterylosis, *n.*, the arrangement and locations of feathers on the body.

ptilopaedic, *adj.*, young that at hatching are well covered with down; distinguished from **psilopaedic**; see also **precocial**.

ptilosis, *n.*, plumage.

pubis, *n.*, slender needlelike bone below the ischium (lower pelvic bone), forming part of the acetabulum (hip socket), separated from the ischium at the anterior end by the obturator foramen.

puffin, one of three species of alcids (auks and their allies, family *Alcidae*). Puffins are medium-size black-and-white water birds with spectacular, large, colored beaks.

pulmocutaneous, *adj.*, describing loss of water by evaporation from the respiratory passages and from the skin.

pygostyle, *n.*, the last six caudal (tail) vertebrae, fused into a plowshare shape, furnishing an anchor for the rectrices (tail feathers).

pyloric stomach, *n.*, a chamber in the alimentary (digestive) tract between the gizzard and the duodenum (small intestine), found in many waterbirds. The function of the pyloric stomach is not known, but it may be related to control or elimination of excessive water intake while feeding.

Qq

quadrate, *n.*, a paired bone of the skull providing the anchor point for the framework that supports and moves the lower mandible.

quail, substantive name for many of the smaller *Phasianidae*, six North American species. Quail are medium-sized, insect- and seed-eating, covey-forming, strikingly plumed game birds.

quaily, colloquial name for the Upland Sandpiper, *Bartramia longicauda*.

quandy, colloquial name for the Oldsquaw, *Clangula hyemalis*.

quill, *n.*, the bare proximal part of the feather shaft; also called the **calamus**.

quinder, colloquial name for some of the diving ducks, *Aythya*, particularly goldeneyes and scaup.

Rr

race, *n.*, a fractional population of a species in which the members are capable of interbreeding with other races, but are distinguished by unique morphological or behavioral characteristics or geographic isolation (for example, Slate-colored, Gray-headed, and Oregon Juncos, which are races of the Dark-eyed Junco, *Junco hyemalis*); same as **subspecies**, **variety**.

rachis, *n.*, the shaft of a feather, which supports the vanes.

radial, *adj.*, pertaining to the radius.

radiation, *n.*, in evolution, divergence of form in adaptation to opportunities, stresses, and niches; the opposite of **convergent evolution**; see also **adaptive radiation**.

radii, *n.*, the barbs of a perfect feather.

radius, *n.*, one of two bones in the forearm of the wing. The radius is the more slender of the two (the other is the ulna).

rail, a member of the rail family *Rallidae*, including coots, gallinules, rails, and soras. Rails are small to medium-sized wading birds; see also Terres, pp. 753-8.

rain bird, *n.*, colloquial name for different species in different areas, including the Black-billed and Yellow-billed Cuckoos, for their habit of often calling just before rainstorms.

rain-goose, colloquial name for the Red-throated Loon, *Gavia stellata*.

rami, *n.*, plural of **ramus**.

ramus, *n.*, *pl.* **rami**, either of two thickened, pronglike ridges extending posteriorly (back) from the tip of a bird's bill, along the lower surface to the base of the lower mandible. The fused anterior (front) portion of the rami forms a ridge known as the gonys, as in a pigeon. Also, the main axis of the barb of a typical feather, often comma-shaped.

range, *n.*, a geographic area within which a species is generally found. Winter range, breeding range, and migratory ranges typically differ for migratory birds.

raptor, *n.*, a bird of prey.

ratite, *adj.*, having a rounded, small sternum (breastbone), typical in flightless birds (for example, emu, Ostrich); see also **carina**.

ratite, *n.*, any of the flightless birds.

razorbill, substantive name for *Alca torda*, a pelagic, duck-sized alcid, the only species in the genus *Alca*; also called the Razor-billed Auk.

recrudescence, *n.*, see **autumnal recrudescence**.

rectrices, *n.*, plural of **rectrix**.

rectrix, *n.*, *pl.* **rectrices**, the strong, conspicuous flight feathers of the tail, occurring in pairs; distinguished from the **tail coverts**, which cover the base of the tail and the base of the rectrices; **[field mark]**. *See illustration, p. v.*

recurved, *adj.*, describing a bill that curves upward at the tip (for example, that of godwits or avocets, family *Recurvirostridae*).

red-back, colloquial name for the Dunlin, *Calidris alpina*, a small shorebird.

redbill, colloquial name for the American Black Oystercatcher, *Haematopus bachmani*, the Royal Tern, *Sterna maxima*, and the Caspian Tern, *Sterna caspia*.

redbird, colloquial name for the Northern Cardinal, *Cardinalis cardinalis*, the Scarlet Tanager, *Piranga olivacea*, and the Summer Tanager, *Piranga rubra*.

redbreast, colloquial name for the American Robin, *Turdus* *migratorius*, the Eastern Bluebird, *Sialia sialis*, and the Red Knot, *Calidris canutus*.

red-hammer, colloquial name for Red-shafted race of Northern Flicker, *Colaptes auratus*, a woodpecker.

redhead, substantive name for *Aythya americana*, a diving duck. Also a colloquial name for the Red-headed Woodpecker, *Melanerpes erythrocephalus*.

redleg, colloquial name for the Black Duck, *Anas rubripes*.

redpoll, substantive name for either of two species of small red finches, the Common Redpoll, *Carduelis flammea*, and the Hoary Redpoll, *Carduelis hornemanni*.

redshank, shortened name for the Spotted Redshank, *Tringa erythropus*, a sandpiper. Also a colloquial name for the Common Tern, *Sterna hirundo*, and Royal Tern, *Sterna maxima*.

redstart, substantive name for two warbler species, the Painted Redstart, *Myioborus pictus*, and the American Redstart, *Setophaga ruticilla*.

red-tail, shortened name for the Red-tailed Hawk, *Buteo jamaicensis*.

redwing, shortened name for the Red-winged Blackbird, *Agelaius phoenicius*.

reed-bird, colloquial name for the Bobolink, *Dolichonyx oryzivorus*.

reeve, a female Ruff, *Philomachus pugnax*, a small sandpiper.

reflected, *adj.*, turned backward.

reflection, *n.*, a color change that appears when a feather faces different angles of light.

refracted, *adj.*, abruptly bent, as if broken.

region, *n.*, any localized portion of the body, such as the anal region or dorsal region.

regurgitation, *n.*, casting up of partly digested food, to feed the young; vomiting pellets of undigestible fur, hair, bones, etc. Also, vomiting of foul smelling oil as a means of defense (done, for example, by fulmars).

relict, *n.*, an isolated population that appears to be a fragment of a former widely distributed population.

remex, *n.*, *pl.* **remiges**, a large quill feather in a wing, a flight feather. The word is usually used in its plural form (remiges). Primary remiges (usually ten) are the largest, outermost wing feathers; secondary remiges (usually nine or ten) compose the balance of the trailing edge of the wing.

remiges, *n.*, plural of **remex**.

renal, *adj.*, pertaining to the kidneys and kidney functions.

reniform, *adj.*, kidney-shaped.

replicate, *adj.*, folded over so as to form a groove or channel.

resident, *adj.*, residing in the same area year-round, not migratory (for example, the Red-breasted Nuthatch, *Sitta canadensis*). Some use the term "summer resident" to denote a population that breeds in an area; see also **sedentary**.

respiratory system, *n.*; see **lungs**; see also Terres, pp. 762-4.

reticulate, *adj.*, describing a podotheca (leg covering) consisting of fine scales; also, marked with cross lines like the meshes of a net.

rhamphotheca, *n.*, the outermost covering of the bill, hornlike in most birds, but softer and leathery in many shorebirds and waterfowl.

rhinal, *adj.*, pertaining to the nose.

rhomboid, *adj.*, lozenge-shaped.

rib, *n.*, a flattened long bone enclosing the chest cavity, articulated with the vertebrae and sternum. In birds ribs are jointed and interconnected to allow flexibility during breathing (since birds do not have diaphragms).

ricebird, colloquial name for the Bobolink, *Dolichonyx oryzivorus*.

rictal, *adj.*, pertaining to the rictus.

rictal bristle, *n.*, short bristles (feathers) located at the base of the bill in some species, especially fly-catching species, which aid in catching insects.

rictus, *n.*, the soft and more fleshy part of a bird's bill near the commissural point (angle of the mouth); part of the tomium (edge of the upper or lower mandible).

rimal, *adj.*, describing feathers making up the eye ring; [field mark].

ring-bill, colloquial name for the Ring-necked Duck, *Aythya collaris*.

ring-neck, shortened name for the Ring-necked Duck, *Aythya collaris*, and the Ring-necked Pheasant, *Phasianus colchicus*.

road-trotter, colloquial name for the Horned Lark, *Eremophila alpestris*.

rock-bird, colloquial name for the Ruddy Turnstone, *Arenaria interpres*.

rockweed bird, colloquial name for the Purple Sandpiper, *Calidris maritima*.

rookery, *n.*, a colony of nests built by birds such as penguins, herons, and crows, named after the English Rook, or crow. Great Blue Herons may build dozens of nests in the adjacent tops of trees in a given rookery.

roost, *n.*, a perch where one or more birds rest at night. Also, a place where flocks or groups of birds sleep together in treetops, marsh reeds, or other safe places.

roosting, *v.*, resting, sleeping, or perching on a roost.

rostrum, *n.*, another name for the bill or beak.

rough-leg, shortened name for the Rough-legged Hawk, *Buteo lagopus*.

ruby-throat, shortened name for the Ruby-throated Hummingbird, *Archilochus colubris*

rudimentary, *adj.*, imperfectly developed, as if only begun.

ruff, a small sandpiper, *Philomachus pugnax*, with a spectacular breeding plumage; also, *adj.*, brownish red.

rugose, *adj.*, wrinkled.

rump, *n.*, the area of a bird's back described as the posterior (rearward) third of the area between the base of the neck and the base of the tail; **[field mark]**. *See illustration, p. v.*

ruptive, *adj.*, describing a pattern of protective coloration with bold markings, such as stripes or spots, that break up the body outline and make the bird harder to see (for eample, the Killdeer, *Charadrius vociferus*, has ruptive coloration with bands that help it blend in with rocky shores). (See Thayer, cited in the bibliography, for the theory that bold, ruptive patterns always function as camouflage. His views are not widely shared but his illustrations are breathtaking.)

Ss

sacral, *adj.*, referring to part of the spinal column between the lumbar and caudal vertebrae, near the tail. In birds, sacral vertebrae are fused to form the synsacrum.

saddleback, colloquial name for the Great Black-backed Gull, *Larus marinus*.

sage hen, colloquial name for the Sage Grouse, *Centrocercus urophasianus*.

sagittate, *adj.*, shaped like an arrowhead.

salt glands, *n.*, supraorbital or nasal glands in aquatic birds that capture and excrete excess salt taken in with food or seawater; observed in thirteen orders of birds.

saltatory, *adj.*, progressing by leaps and bounds; contrast with **ambulatory**, **gradient**.

sandpiper, family name and substantive name of many of the large shorebirds (*Scolopacidae*); see also Terres, pp. 768-807.

sand-runner, colloquial name for the Ruddy Turnstone, *Arenaria interpres*.

sanitizing of nests, *v.*, removing excreta of the young from the nests.

sap-feeding, *n.*, feeding by many species on sap oozing from holes drilled by sapsuckers and Downy Woodpeckers. Some birds, including many other than the woodpeckers, also feed on insects caught in the sap dripping from the woodpeckers' holes.

sapsucker, substantive name for three species of woodpeckers, *Sphyrapicus* spp., Williamson's Sapsucker, Red-breasted

Sapsucker, and the Rednaped Sapsucker and the Yellow-bellied Sapsucker, the latter two being subspecies of one species.

sawbill, colloquial name for any of the mergansers, *Mergus* spp.

scabrous, *adj.*, scabby or scaly, when referring to legs and feet.

scalloped, *adj.*, cut along the edge or border in circular or shell-shaped segments.

scapula, *n.*, a bone lying parallel to the spinal column, resting upon the ribs and articulating with the bones of the pectoral girdle.

scapular, *n.*, a shoulder feather; *adj.*, pertaining to the shoulder region; **[field mark]**. *See illustration, p. v.*

scapular region, *n.*, the usually well-defined lengthwise area of feathers overlying the shoulder blade; see also **interscapulars**.

scapulars, *n.*, the feathers of the shoulder; **[field mark]**.

scavengers, *n.*, birds that clean up dead animals and other wastes on land and water, including hawks, vultures, many of the gulls and their allies, shearwaters and their allies, crows and their allies, and others.

schizochroism, *n.*, a rare condition of abnormal paleness resulting from absence of a darker pigment.

schizorhinal, *adj.*, having nostrils that have decidedly slitlike or triangular rear margins.

scoggin, colloquial name for a heron or bittern (*Ardeidae*).

scoldenore, colloquial name for the Oldsquaw, *Clangula hyemalis*.

scolopacine, *adj.*, snipelike or pertaining to the snipe family (*Scolopacidae*).

scutellate, *adj.*, describing a podotheca (unfeathered leg) with large and often overlapping scales.

scutellum, *n.*, *pl.* **scutella**, overlapping horny scales on the exterior of the tarsus (foot) and toes of most birds.

scutes, *n.*, large scales on the front surface of the tarsus (foot) in some birds.

scutiform, *adj.*, shield-shaped.

seabird, imprecise term often used to denote marine or pelagic birds.

sea-crow, colloquial name for the Razorbill, *Alca torda*, the American Coot, *Fulica americana*, and the American Oystercatcher, *Haematopus palliatus*.

sea-dog, colloquial name for the Black Skimmer, *Rynchops niger*; because of its call, which sounds like a dog barking.

sea eagles, colloquial name for terns.

sea-goose, colloquial name for phalaropes (*Phalaropodidae*).

seagull, common name for gulls (*Laridae*, *Larus* spp.), whether marine or inland. Ornithologists usually use the shorter "gull."

sea horse, colloquial name for the Northern Fulmar, *Fulmarus glacialis*.

sea mouse, colloquial name for the Harlequin Duck, *Histrionicus histrionicus*, because of its squeaky call.

sea parrot, colloquial name for puffins (*Alcidae*).

sea-snipe, colloquial name for phalaropes (*Phalaropodidae*).

search image, *n.*, learned fixation on an abundant food source, such as a specific insect hatch, and pursuit of that source until exhausted. A search image is learned as a result of past rewards or penalties after eating.

sea-swallow, common name for terns (*Laridae*, *Sterninae*).

secondaries, *n.*, remiges (flight feathers) on the trailing edge of the wing, proximal (closer to the body) from the primaries. There are usually nine or ten secondaries, numbered from the outside in, and attached to the ulna (wing bone). The upper surface of the secondaries is the speculum in ducks; **[field mark]**. *See illustration, pp. v, 80.*

secondary coverts, *n.*, numerous small wing feathers overlying and protecting the bases of the secondary flight feathers, divided into lesser secondary coverts, median secondary coverts, and greater secondary coverts. The secondary coverts often display field marks; **[field mark]**. *See illustration, p. 80.*

secondary quills, *n.*, long feathers of the forearm, which in the spread wing appear in a continuous row with the primaries.

secondary sexual characteristics, *n.*, external differences between the sexes (such as bright colors, combs, spurs, bright skin patches, long tails, etc.), used by females to assess the fitness of potential breeding mates (in polygamous species); **[field marks]**.

sedentary, *adj.*, nonmigratory; see also **resident**.

sedge hen, colloquial name for the Clapper Rail, *Rallus longirostris*.

seesaw, colloquial name for the Spotted Sandpiper, *Actitis macularia*.

segmentation, *n.*, division into parts or segments.

sematic, *adj.*, describing behavior or coloration that signals a warning or attractive clue. Includes **allosematic**, adventitiously derived from association with other species; **aposematic**, protective coloration; **episematic**, aiding recognition; **gamosematic**, aiding pair recognition; **parasematic**, deflecting attention; **proepisematic**, markings that help to maintain recognition and contact in groups.

semicircular, *adj.*, divided into a shape like one-half of a circle.

semicircular canals, *n.*, organs in the inner ear that help to maintain balance and equilibrium, including in flight.

semipalmate, *adj.*, describing feet with small webs linking the forward three toes; distinguished from **palmate** feet in which the webs extend the full length of the toes, see also **fissipalmate**, **totipalmate**. *See illustration, p. 97.*

semiplumes, *n.*, downy feathers found under contour (external) feathers, intermediate between contour feathers and down, with the rachis (shaft) longer than the barbs; used for insulation.

septum, *n.*, a partition, such as between nasal cavities.

serrate, *adj.*, describing a bill with sawlike tomia (cutting edges) (as found in mergansers, *Mergus* spp.).

setaceous, *adj.*, bristly.

setiform, *adj.*, bristlelike.

sewick, another name for the Least Flycatcher, *Empidonax minimus*.

sexual characteristics, *n.*, primary characteristics that distinguish the sexes, such as the sexual organs, testes, and ovaries; see also **secondary sexual characteristics**.

sexual dimorphism, *n.*, differences in size, color, plumage, and markings between the sexes in mature birds; see **dimorphism, sexual**.

sex role reversal, *n.*, the practice of courtship by the female and incubation by the male, found in several species (for example, Wilson's Phalarope, *Phalaropus tricolor*, in which the female is brightly colored and pursues the male in courtship); see also **polyandry**.

shaft, *n.*, the midrib of a feather.

shag, colloquial name for cormorants (*Phalacrocoracidae*).

shank, *n.*, the tarsus, the straight scaly or smooth part of a bird's foot.

sharp-shin, shortened name for the Sharp-shinned Hawk, *Accipiter striatus*.

sharptail, shortened name for the Sharp-tailed Grouse, *Tympanuchus phasianellus*.

shearwater, family and substantive name for pelagic birds including the fulmars, shearwaters, and petrels (*Procellaridae*); see also Terres, pp. 813-9.

sheldrake, colloquial name for shelducks, Canvasbacks, or mergansers.

shorebird, name for many members of the order *Charadriiformes*, including sandpipers, plovers, woodcock, snipe, curlews, and many more; called "waders" in Great Britain.

short-neck, colloquial name for the Pectoral Sandpiper, *Calidris melanotos*.

short white, colloquial name for the Snowy Egret, *Egretta thula*, by plume hunters.

shot-pouch, colloquial name for the Ruddy Duck, *Oxyura jamaicensis*, for its legendary resistance to shot.

shoveler, shortened name for the Northern Shoveler, *Anas clypeata*.

shrike, family and substantive name for aggressive insect and small bird hunters of the family *Laniidae*, with heavy beaks, black masks, short wings with white markings, and dark tails with white outer feathers.

sibilant, *adj.*, hissing.

siblicide, *n.*, killing of a nestmate by another to eliminate competition for food. Siblicide is more common in nests with only two or three chicks; obligate siblicide is common in eagles and boobies, in which the larger nestling almost always kills the smaller; see **brood reduction**.

sickle-bill, colloquial name for the Long-billed Curlew, *Numenius americanus*, one of the largest shorebirds.

silver ternlet, colloquial name for the Least Tern, *Sterna antillarum*.

silver tongue, colloquial name for the Song Sparrow, *Melospiza melodia*.

simpleton, colloquial name for the Dunlin, *Calidris alpina*, a small shorebird.

sinuate, *adj.*, curved. Refers to a feather with an edge that is gradually cut away.

sincipital, *adj.*, pertaining to the **sinciput**, the fore-part of the skull.

sinciput, *n.*, the forward half of the pileum (head); includes the forehead and the crown.

single-brooded, *adj.*, describing species that attempt to raise only one brood to independence during each breeding season. Most birds will attempt to nest again if their first nest is destroyed before the young fledge (leave the nest).

site tenacity, *n.*, the tendency of successive generations to reuse traditional nest sites and foraging or roosting sites; also called **philopatry**, or site fidelity.

sizzle-britches, colloquial name for the Common Goldeneye, *Bucephala clangula*, for its high-speed, whistling flight.

skeleton, *n.*, the bony and cartilaginous framework that protects the brain and internal organs, supports and is integrated with air sacs, and supports the wings and tail; see also Campbell & Lack, pp. 543-6, and Terres, pp. 824-6. *See illustrations, pp. 8, 9.*

skimmer, family and substantive name for several species of medium-size, gull-like, strong fliers (*Rynchopidae*) with a lower mandible substantially longer than the upper, used to skim the surface of the water for small fish and other prey.

skin, *n.*, the typically thin, two-layer outer or integumentary covering of the body, usually covered with feathers in birds.

skua, subfamily and substantive name for large pelagic birds (Subfamily *stercorariinae*, family *Laridae*).

skull, *n.*, the bones that protect the eyes and brain and support the bill; see Campbell & Lack, pp. 549-51. *See illustration, p. 125.*

skunk bird, colloquial name for the Bobolink, *Dolichonyx oryzivorus*.

Skull with Tongue Structure
(Red-bellied Woodpecker)

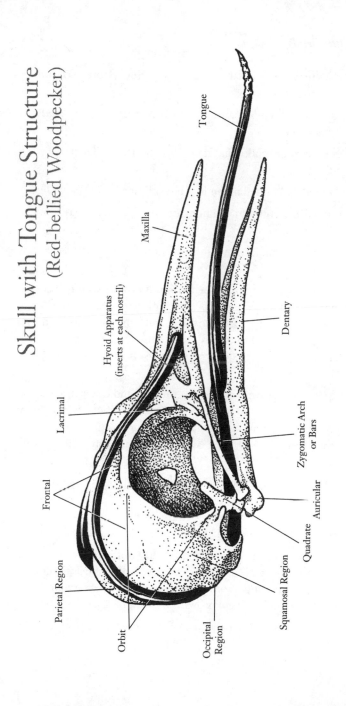

Tongue

Maxilla

Dentary

Hyoid Apparatus
(inserts at each nostril)

Lacrimal

Zygomatic Arch
or Bars

Auricular

Frontal

Quadrate

Parietal Region

Squamosal Region

Orbit

Occipital
Region

skunk-head, colloquial name for the Surf Scoter, *Melanitta perspicillata*.

sky-gazer, colloquial name for the American Bittern, *Botaurus lentiginosus*.

sleepy brother, colloquial name for the Ruddy Duck, *Oxyura jamaicensis*.

snakebird, colloquial name for the Anhinga, *Anhinga anhinga*.

snake killer, colloquial name for the Greater Roadrunner, *Geococcyx californianus*.

snowbird, colloquial name for the Snow Bunting, *Plectrophenax nivalis*.

sonagrams, *n.*, (sometimes spelled **sonograms**) two-dimensional diagrams of song frequency and timing of notes or calls, with frequency displayed on one axis and time (duration) on the other, often used to differentiate closely related species; also called sonograph or spectrograph; see also Thomson, pp. 740-50.

song, *n.*, any of a wide variety of musical and other utterances, used to identify and protect territory, attract mates, maintain groups, call young, and maybe just express emotion; see also Thomson, pp. 739-50; Campbell & Lack, pp. 629-34; and Terres, pp. 833-5.

songbirds, *n.*, commonly used to denote all of the members of the order of perching birds, *Passeriformes*, also called passerines. Some limit the term to the better singers, especially the finch, tanager, thrush, mimid, warbler, and wren families.

sparrow, one of many members of the subfamily *Emberizinae*, family *Emberizidae*. Sparrows are seed-eating birds that often flock; many sing. Some sparrows have spectacular head markings, and all have brown, streaked backs.

sparrow hawk, alternate name of the American Kestrel, *Falco sparverius*.

spatulate, *adj.*, spatula-shaped. Refers to a bill that is widened or depressed near the tip (for example, that of the Northern Shoveler, *Anas clypeata*).

speciation, *n.*, the process by which new species gradually evolve in response to environmental factors; see also Thomson, pp. 770-4.

species, *n.*, in taxonomy, a population of interbreeding individuals, possessing common characteristics distinguishing it from other similar populations and generally reproductively isolated from other populations.

speckle-belly, colloquial name for the White-fronted Goose, *Anser albifrons*.

speckle-cheek, colloquial name for any of the several ladder-backed woodpecker species (*Picidae*).

speculum, *n.*, the metallic or brightly colored patch comprising the upper surface of the secondary flight feathers (for example, that of the Mallard, *Anas platyrhynchos*); [field mark].

spike-bill, colloquial name for the Marbled Godwit, *Limosa fedoa*.

spike-tail, colloquial name for the Northern Pintail duck, *Anas acuta*.

spinose, spinous, *adj.*, having spines; sometimes said of a mucronate (spine-tipped) feather.

spoonbill, shortened name for the Roseate Spoonbill, *Ajaia ajaja*; also a common name for the Northern Shoveler, *Anas clypeata*, and the Spoonbill Sandpiper, *Eurynorhynchus pygmeus*.

sp., *pl.* **spp.**, abbreviation for species.

sprig, colloquial name for the Northern Pintail duck, *Anas acuta*.

spur, *n.*, a sharp, horny growth on the rear of the tarsus in some game birds (for example, the Ring-necked Pheasant, *Phasianus colchicus*).

squab, *n.*, a young dove or pigeon (*Columbidae*).

squamose, squamous, *adj.*, scalelike or scaly.

squaw, shortened name for the Oldsquaw, *Bucephala clangula*.

stage-driver, colloquial name for the King Rail, *Rallus elegans*.

stake-driver, colloquial name for the American Bittern, *Botaurus lentiginosus*.

stenophagous, *adj.*, describing species that are limited to a narrow range of diets (for example, hummingbirds, which eat only nectar); see also **monophagous** and **euryphagous**.

sterile, *adj.*, unfruitful, barren, unable to reproduce.

sternum, *n.*, the breastbone, a flattened vertical bone with a visible keel providing an anchor for the flight muscles of the breast.

stiff-tail, another name for the Ruddy Duck, *Oxyura jamaicensis*.

stint, common name in Great Britain for many of the small sandpipers.

stipule, *n.*, a newly sprouted feather.

stomach oil, *n.*, foul-smelling liquid vomited by some seabirds (for example, the Northern Fulmar) for defense.

stork, family and substantive name for large marsh birds (*Ciconiidae*).

storm-petrel, family and substantive name for four species of small petrels (*Hydrobatidae*), pelagic, surface-feeding birds.

stragulum, *n.*, the mantle (back and upper wings); also called pallium.

streak, *n.*, a narrow longitudinal color mark or stripe.

stria, *n.*, a streak.

striate, *adj.*, streaked.

stripe, *n.*, a broad longitudinal color mark or broad streak.

structural coloration, *n.*, apparent color resulting from interference with light waves by the structure of overlapping barbules containing melanin granules which absorb parts of the spectrum which are not reflected; often described as showing **iridescent colors**; see also **iridescence**.

struthionine, *adj.*, pertaining to or having the characteristics of the ostriches (*Struthiones*).

strutting ground, *n.*, an area where males of a species display in a group to attract and mate with females; see also **lek**.

subadult, *n.*, a young (not adult) bird of a species that requires more than one year to reach breeding maturity.

subbasal, *adj.*, near the base.

subcaudal, *adj.*, beneath the tail.

subclass, *n.*, a group between class and order in taxonomic rank.

subfamily, *n.*, taxonomic classification next below family and immediately above genus; see Appendices II and III.

subgenus, *n.*, a subdivision of genus, frequently not recognized by name except in the grouping of species.

submalar, *adj.*, beneath the malar region (cheeks).

suborbital, *adj.*, beneath the eyes.

suborder, *n.*, taxonomic classification next below an order and above a family; see **orders**; see Appendices II and III.

subspecies, *n.*, taxonomic classification immediately below species. A subspecies is morphologically, physiologically, or behaviorally distinct and geographically separate (in terms of habitat or range or, more narrowly, breeding habitat or range) from other members of the species, but capable of successful interbreeding with other subspecies when they do occur in the same area; also called **race** or **variety**.

superciliary line, *n.*, a line or stripe running from front to back above the eye, sometimes fine, which may resemble an eyebrow (such as that in the Northern Goshawk); **[field mark]**. *See illustration, p. 137.*

supercilium, *n.*, the eyebrow; also known as the **superciliary line**; [**field mark**]. *See illustration, p. 137.*

superfamily, *n.*, taxonomic classification ranking next above a family and below suborder, used when two or more families are especially closely related.

superior, *adj.*, lying over; topmost or uppermost.

superorder, *n.*, rarely used taxonomic classification that is below class and above order.

superspecies, *n.*, unofficial taxonomic classification of two or more highly similar species, but not similar enough to be considered subspecies, separated geographically but which would likely interbreed if brought together; see also **allospecies**.

supinating, *v.*, rotating the wing's leading edge up for braking; opposite of **pronating**.

supra-auricular, *adj.*, above the auriculars (ear coverts).

supraloral, *adj.*, above the lores.

supraorbital, *adj.*, above the eyes.

supraorbital gland, *n.*, nasal glands that remove excess salt from birds that drink seawater; see **salt gland**.

supraorbital ridge, *n.*, a bony ridge over the top of the eye (found in accipiters, for example).

swallow, family and substantive name for fast, insect-catching birds (*Hirundinidae*) with long wings, forked tails, short necks, and wide mouths; see also Terres, pp. 863-7.

swamp angel, colloquial name for members of the thrush family, *Turdidae*, subfamily *Turdinae*, subfamily *Muscicapidae*.

swan, substantive name for any of several Old World species and two North American species of large, white, long-necked waterfowl, genus *Cygnus*, subfamily *Anserinae*, family *Anatidae*.

swift, family and substantive name for cliff-nesting, noisy, insectivorous, swift-flying birds (*Apodidae*), with four North American species.

swollen, *adj.*, a bill with mandibles that are convex at the sides (such as those of tanagers, *Emberizidae thraupinae*).

sympatric, *adj.*, describing two species (often two highly similar species) whose breeding ranges overlap but who remain reproductively isolated due to other characteristics; compare to **allopatric**.

synaposematic, *adj.*, describing a warning signal shared with other species; see also **aposematic**.

syndactyl, **syndactlyous**, *adj.*, feet with three toes facing to the front and one facing back, but with the second and third toes fused for much of their length (for example, in kingfishers, *Alcedinidae*). *See illustration, p. 62.*

synsacrum, *n.*, the fused-together series of thoracic, lumbar, and sacral vertebrae in the pelvic area.

syrinx, *n.*, voice organ, located where the trachea divides, comprising a system of muscles, valves, and membranes.

systematics, *n.*, the study of physiological, physical, behavioral, genetic, and biochemical relationships among organisms, to classify and name organisms and groups of organisms; see also **classification**, **taxonomy**, **name**, **nomenclature**.

Tt

tail, *n.*, the tail feathers **(rectrices)** used for flight, display, and perching; growing from the **pygostyle**. *See illustration, p. v.*

tail coverts, *n.*, small feathers that cover the bases of the large tail feathers. The uppertail coverts make up the rump above the tail (as in the peacock and paradise trogon); the undertail coverts form the crissum below the tail; **[field marks]**. *See illustration, p. v.*

talons, *n.*, sharp claws of birds of prey; see also **feet**. *See illustration, p. 97.*

tanager, family name for the *Thraupidae*, now subfamily *Thraupinae* of the family *Emberizidae*.

tarsal, *adj.*, referring to the bones of the intertarsal joint (ankle).

tarsometatarsus, *n.*, the bone of the tarsus (lower leg), formed by a fusion of the tarsal and metatarsal elements.

tarsus, *n.*, the third (distal) segment of the leg, between the crus (lower leg, or shank) and the toes, containing the tarsometatarsus bone, typically scaly all over and feathered only at the upper joint; analogous to the human foot between the ankle and the toes.

tawny, *adj.*, the color of tanned leather.

taxon, *n.*, *pl.* **taxa**, a category used in classification and naming of biological entities. The primary taxa in current use are **kingdom**, **phylum**, **class**, **order**, **family**, **genus**, **species**, and **subspecies**; see appendices.

taxonomy, *n.*, the science of classification (sorting, dividing, and grouping) and naming plants and animals; see also **systematics**, **classification**, **nomenclature**, **names**; see appendices.

tear glands, *n.*, glands that secrete oils to protect the eyes from salt water; also called **Harderian glands** or **lachrymal glands**.

tectrix, *n.*, *pl.* **tectrices**, a small feather that covers the base of a flight feather in the wing or tail; same as **covert**.

teleological, *adj.*, pertaining to a modification resulting from necessary adaptation. Thus, the naked head and other vulturine aspects of the Old World vultures (*Falconidae*) and those of the New World vultures (*Cathartidae*) are teleological because the birds' mode of living (as scavengers) requires a certain body structure, evolving differently in each hemisphere.

teleology, *n.*, the scientific study of adaptation.

teleoptile, *n.*, any of six types of feathers of adult birds, including **contour feathers**, **semiplumes**, **down**, **filoplumes**, **bristles**, and **powder-down feathers**; contrast **neossoptiles**.

temporal, *adj.*, pertaining to the temples.

temporal canthus, *n.*, the posterior corner of the eye; see **canthus**.

terete, *adj.*, a bill that is generally circular in cross-section viewed both frontally and laterally (for example, the bills of hummingbirds, *Trochilidae*).

terminal, *adj.*, at the end.

tern, any of numerous streamlined, long-winged, forked-tailed species of the subfamily *Sterninae*, family *Laridae*, which skim and dive into coastal and inland waters for fish and insects.

territory, *n.*, an area within feeding, breeding, or nesting habitat defended by the male or by the breeding pair or, rarely, by an unmated female.

tertial, *adj.*, referring to tertiary flight feathers.

tertiaries, *n.*, the innermost feathers on the upper surface of the wing, proximal (inboard) from the secondaries and posterior to (behind) the scapulars; not remiges (flight feathers), tertiaries are attached to the brachium (the proximal part of the wing); also called **tertials**. *See illustration, p. 148.*

testis, *n.*, *pl.* **testes**, the male gonad.

tetradactyl, *adj.*, four-toed, as most birds are.

theca, *n.*, a sheathlike covering of some type of hard or horny material (for example, the **podotheca**, covering the tarsus, or the **rhamphotheca**, covering the bill).

thecodonts, *n.*, precursors to the dinosaurs and reptiles, some of whom had birdlike features such as elongated scales, clavicles fused into a furcula (wishbone), and a birdlike skull; see also **pterosaurs**.

thermoregulation, *n.*, regulation of body temperature within an optimal range by increasing metabolism during cold and evaporating body moisture during heat, and by behavior that increases or reduces heat loss from feet and legs, unfeathered areas, and the respiratory system; see also **gular fluttering**, **heat balance**, **gaping**, **panting**.

thigh, *n.*, the proximal segment of the leg containing the femur, above the crus or shank (drumstick).

thistle-bird, colloquial name for the American Goldfinch, *Carduelis tristis*, which uses thistles for feed and nesting material.

thoracic, *adj.*, pertaining to the thorax.

thoracic vertebrae, *n.*, vertebrae occurring posterior to (behind) the cervical vertebrae and anterior to the lumbar and sacral vertebrae, often fused to form the synsacrum (pelvic girdle) of birds.

thorax, *n.*, the chest and the cavity containing the heart and lungs.

thrasher, substantive name for several of the species of the family *Mimidae*. There are eight North American species of thrasher, with long tails, long decurved bills, strong voices, and the ability to mimic other birds' calls.

throat, *n.*, the external region below the chin, including the **gular region** and the **jugulum**; **[field mark]**. *See illustration, p. v.*

throat-cut, colloquial name for the Rose-breasted Grosbeak, *Pheucticus ludovicianus.*

thrush, family name and substantive name for several species of the *Turdinae*, family *Muscicapidae*. Thrushes are mostly shy with spotted breasts, dull markings, good voices, and a preference for thick cover; see also Terres, pp. 884-922.

thunder pumper, colloquial name for the American Bittern, *Botaurus lentiginosus*, for its low-pitched call.

tibia, *n.*, see **tibiotarsus**.

tibial, *adj.*, pertaining to the tibiotarsus.

tibiotarsus, *n.*, the principal long bone between the knee joint and the ankle joint, running parallel to the thinner and shorter fibula; also called the **tibia**.

tip-up, colloquial name for the Solitary Sandpiper, *Tringa solitaria*, the Spotted Sandpiper, *Actitis macularia*, or the Greater Yellowlegs, *Tringa melanoleuca*.

tit, shortened name for any member of the titmouse and chickadee family, *Paridae*; see also Terres, pp. 924-8.

titmouse, substantive name for any of three North American species of the *Paridae*, small woodland birds with crests, which resemble chickadees.

tobacco bird, colloquial name for the Common Ground Dove, *Columbina passerina.*

tomial tooth, *n.*, a notch in the tomium of the upper mandible in falcons and shrikes; **[field mark]**.

tomium, *n.*, *pl.* **tomia**, the cutting edge on each side of either the upper or lower part of a bird's bill (mandible), described respectively as the upper mandibular tomia or the lower mandibular tomia.

tomtit, colloquial name for the Tufted Titmouse, *Parus bicolor*.

tooth, egg, *n.*, a calcareous (hardened) sharp growth at the tip of the bill of the embryonic chick, used by hatching birds to "pip" a hole in the egg.

topography, *n.*, the collective description of the exterior surfaces of birds for aid in identification.

topsy-turvy bird, colloquial name for members of the nuthatch family (*Sittidae*).

torpidity, *n.*, the temporary (for a day or two) abandonment of homeothermy (warm-bloodedness), when body temperature is lowered to conserve energy during periods of low temperature or low food availability (as seen, for example, in poor-wills, swifts, swallows, and other insect-eaters); distinguished from **hibernation**, which is a seasonal process.

totipalmate, *adj.*, describing a foot with all four toes connected by webbing (for example, the feet of gannets, boobies, pelicans, and cormorants). *See illustration, p. 97.*

towhee, one of four species of the genus *Pipilo*, subfamily *Emberizinae*, family *Emberizidae*. Towhees have long tails and thick bills, and are ground-feeding, tail-pumping, hop-and-kicking birds, several of which have well-known songs.

trachea, *n.*, the windpipe, including, anterior, the **larynx**, which does not function in making sounds, and, posterior, the **syrinx**, which is used to make sounds.

tracheal bulla, *n.*, an enlargement of the trachea above the syrinx, used as a sound chamber in ducks.

tramp, colloquial name for the introduced House Sparrow, *Passer domesticus*.

transient, *adj.*, a species or individual that crosses a region on the way to and from winter and breeding habitats, but that does not normally breed or winter in that region; same as **vagrant** or **visitor**; compare **resident**.

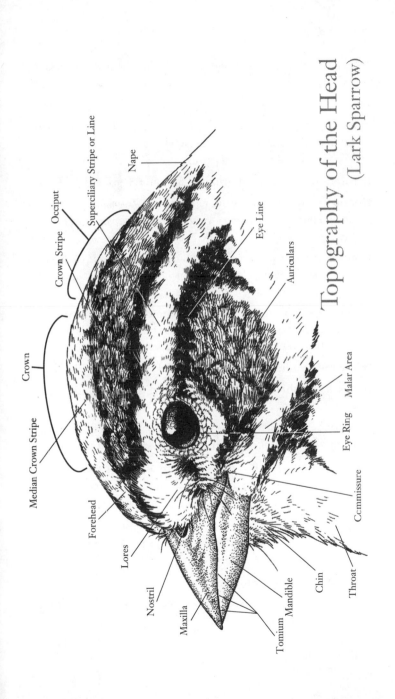

Topography of the Head
(Lark Sparrow)

Nape

Superciliary Stripe or Line

Occiput

Crown Stripe

Crown

Median Crown Stripe

Forehead

Lores

Nostril

Maxilla

Tomium

Mandible

Chin

Throat

Commissure

Eye Ring

Malar Area

Auriculars

Eye Line

tree-girdler, colloquial name for the Yellow-bellied Sapsucker, *Sphyrapicus varius*.

tribe, *n.*, a taxonomic category beneath family and above genus.

tridactyl, *adj.*, three-toed, with two toes in the front and one in the rear (for example, the tridactyl foot of the Three-toed Woodpecker, *Picoides tridactylus*).

trituration, *n.*, the act of grinding food in the gizzard.

trogon, family and substantive name for the *Trogonidae*, of which one member, the Elegant Trogon, *Trogon elegans*, nests near the Rio Grande valley on the Mexican border.

troupials, family name for the blackbird and oriole group formerly known as the family *Icteridae*, now classified as the subfamily *Icterinae* of the family *Emberizidae*; see **icterids**.

tubenoses, common name for members of the order *Procellariiformes* (oceanic birds), for their paired breathing tubes along the ridge of the upper mandible.

tubinares, another name for tubenoses.

tunics, *n.*, the three membrane layers enclosing the globe of the eye.

turnstone, shortened name for the Ruddy Turnstone, *Arenaria interpres*, or the Black Turnstone, *Arenaria melanocephala*.

turkey, substantive name of two species of *Meleagrididae*.

turkey, water, colloquial name for anhingas (*Anhingidae*) or cormorants (*Phalacrocoracidae*).

tympaniform membranes, *n.*, membranes of the syrinx (the voice organ), which vibrate as air is forced through the bronchus to produce sound.

tympanum, *n.*, eardrum.

typical, *adj.*, agreeing closely with characters assigned to a group, genus, or species.

tyrant, family name for the tyrant-flycatchers (*Tyrannidae*); see **flycatchers**.

Uu

ulna, *n.*, the more sturdy and curved, outside member of the paired bones in the forearm of the wing; the other is the **radius**.

ulnar, *adj.*, pertaining to the ulna.

ulnare, *n.*, one of the fused proximal carpal bones in the "wrist" joint of the wing.

umbilicus, *n.*, an opening in the shaft of a feather whereby the feather is supplied with nutrients during feather growth.

unciform, uncinate, *adj.*, hooked.

undulate, *adj.*, marked with wavy lines.

uniparous, *adj.*, producing only one egg (for example, petrels and auks).

urates, *n.*, insoluble salts of uric metabolic wastes, stabilized for storage in the outer membrane of the developing egg; see also **allantois**.

uric acid, *n.*, concentrated wastes from metabolism, excreted as a white semisolid with the feces. This method of excretion, unique to birds and reptiles, conserves water.

urodeum, *n.*, a compartment in the cloaca in which eggs and sperm are stored and fertilization occurs; see also **oviduct**.

urohydrosis, *n.*, the process of excreting liquid (waste) upon the legs to enhance cooling by evaporation, practiced by vultures and storks to dissipate heat.

uropygial, *adj.*, pertaining to the rump.

uropygial gland, *n.*, the oil gland located just above the base of the tail feathers in most birds, used for preening and oiling the feathers; also called **oil gland** or **preen gland**.

uropygium, *n.*, the rump.

uterus, *n.*, the region of the oviduct in which the shell is deposited around the egg.

Vv

vagina, *n.*, the region of the oviduct near the cloaca in which the egg is held until laying.

vagrant, *n.*, name for a bird that has migrated outside of its normal migration range; same as **visitor** or **transient**; see also **irruption**.

vane, *n.*, the organized series of barbs on each side of the rachis (shaft) of a typical feather, forming a smooth plane because of interlocking of barbs; also called the **vexillum**.

vaned feather, *n.*, a contour or flight feather with a more sturdy rachis (shaft) than a plume or filoplume.

variety, *n.*, a term for a domesticated breed, or a subspecies of wild birds; see **race**, **subspecies**.

vas deferens, *n.*, part of the male reproductive system, a tube that delivers sperm from the testes to the seminal vesicle, which connects to the cloaca.

veery, *Catharus fuscescens*, a small woodland thrush.

vent, *n.*, the cloaca; used for excretion of wastes and sexual and reproductive functions.

ventral, *adj.*, in anatomy, on, of, or toward the belly; distinguished from **dorsal**.

ventral region, *n.*, the feathers surrounding or immediately adjacent to the vent.

ventricles, *n.*, the larger two chambers of the heart; also called **atria**.

ventriculus, *n.*, the gizzard, an organ that grinds food to aid digestion.

vermiculate, *adj.*, marked with irregular fine lines like the tracks of worms (for example, the back feathers on mature drake gadwalls, *Anas strepera*).

vermiform, *adj.*, worm-shaped (for example, a woodpecker's tongue).

vernal, *adj.*, pertaining to spring.

verrucose, verrucous, *adj.*, warty.

vertebrates, *n.*, the highest level of development in the animal kingdom. The subphylum *Vertebrata* of the phylum *Chordata*, vertebrates include sharks, fish, reptiles, amphibians, mammals, and birds.

vertex, *n.*, the crown or central part of the pileum (head).

vestibule, *n.*, an area of the inner ear.

vexillum, *n.*, another name for the vane of a feather.

viable population size, *n.*, the minimum number of individuals (of a variety, population, or species) below which successful breeding and reproduction cannot keep pace with death losses to maintain the population through time. For example, one hundred surviving Heath Hens, *Tympanuchus cupido pinnatus*, could not keep pace with predation and nest losses and thus became extinct in 1932. The hundred birds were not a viable population.

vireo, substantive name for most species of the family *Vireonidae*; with eleven North American species. Vireos are insectivorous, shy, subtly marked, well-voiced, and plagued severely by cowbird parasitism; see also Terres, pp. 950-5.

visitor, *n.*, another name for a vagrant or transient.

vitelline membrane, *n.*, the membrane of the developing egg that encloses the yolk.

vitreous, *adj.*, pertaining to the interior of the eye.

viviparity, *n.*, giving birth to developed young; in contrast to

oviparity, laying eggs in which the young develop outside the body of the mother.

viviparous, *adj.*, describing a taxonomic group that gives birth to developed young; compare to **oviparous**.

vulture, substantive name for any of the three North American species of the *Cathartidae*, large, dark, carrion-eating birds of prey; sometimes loosely used to describe eagles or large hawks.

Ww

wader, common name for any shorebird in Great Britain.

wagtail, substantive name for any of several Eurasian members of the pipit family (*Motacillidae*).

warbler, family name and substantive name for most species of the *Parulinae*, a large subfamily of the *Emberizidae* in North America. Also, several species of the *Sylviinae*, family *Muscicapidae*, Old World warblers; see **wood-warbler**; see also Terres, pp. 961-1001.

water balance, *n.*, maintenance of necessary water in the blood and cells by drinking surface water or extracting water from foods, resorbing water filtered through the kidneys, excretion of semisolid uric acid instead of liquid urine, secretion of excess salt through the salt glands (in oceanic birds), and adjustment of metabolism.

water bird, loosely used general term for birds that spend substantial time around water. The term is often used to refer to shorebirds, waterfowl, or sea birds.

water dance, *n.*, a display on, and sometimes under, water by the murres, auklets, and other alcids (*Alcidae*), loons (*Gaviidae)*, and grebes (*Podicipedidae*).

waterfowl, collective term for ducks, geese, and swans (*Anatidae)*; called **wildfowl** in Great Britain.

water hen, colloquial name for coots and gallinules (*Rallidae*).

water ouzel, alternate name for the American Dipper, *Cinclus mexicanus*.

water requirements, *n.*; see **water balance**.

waterthrush, substantive name of two *Seiurus* spp. of warblers (*Parulinae*).

144

water turkey, colloquial name for anhingas (*Anhingidae*) and cormorants (*Phalacrocoracidae*), order *Pelecaniformes*.

water witches, colloquial name for some of the grebes (*Podicipedidae*).

wattle, *n.*, bare, fleshy, sometimes brightly colored folded skin hanging from the lower bill or chin area, often seen in domestic fowl, turkeys, and a few domestic geese; also called a **dewlap**; see also **lappet**.

waxwing, substantive name for two North American and one European species of *Bombycilla* of the monotypic family *Bombycillidae*. Waxwings are handsome, crested, colorful, gregarious, short-tailed birds that eat berries and make a buzzing call.

weaverbird, common name for members of an Old World family *Ploceidae*, including the introduced pests, House Sparrow and Eurasian Tree Sparrow (not to be confused with the American Tree Sparrow, *Spizella arborea*).

whale-bird, colloquial name for phalaropes or shearwaters.

wheatear, substantive name of various *Oenanthe* spp., of which only one, the Northern Wheatear, *Oenanthe oenanthe*, is found in North America.

wheep, colloquial name for the Great Crested Flycatcher, *Myiarchus crinitus*.

whimbrel, a large sandpiper with long decurved bill, *Numenius phaeopus*.

whip-poor-will, one of the goatsuckers, *Caprimulgus vociferus*.

whip-tail, colloquial name for the jaegers, family *Laridae*, subfamily *Stercorariinae*.

whiskey-jack, colloquial name for the Gray Jay, *Perisoreus canadensis*.

whistler, colloquial name for either of the two goldeneye duck species *Bucephala* spp., or the American Woodcock, *Scolopax minor*.

whistle-wing, colloquial name for goldeneyes, *Bucephala spp.*

whiteback, colloquial name for the Canvasback, *Aythya valisineria*.

white-bill, colloquial name for the Dark-eyed Junco, *Junco hyemalis*.

whitebird, common name for the Snow Bunting, *Plectrophenax nivalis*.

white hagdon, colloquial name for the Northern Fulmar, *Fulmarus glacialis*.

white ring-neck, colloquial name for the Piping Plover, *Charadrius melodus*.

whitethroat, shortened name for the White-throated Sparrow, *Zonotrichia albicollis*.

white-wing, shortened name for the White-winged Dove, *Zenaida asiatica*. Also the colloquial name for the White-winged Scoter, *Melanitta fusca*.

whitey, colloquial name for the Sanderling, *Calidris alba*.

whooper, shortened name for the Whooping Crane, *Grus americana*. Also the shortened name for the European Whooper Swan, *Cygnus cygnus*.

wigeon, the American Wigeon, *Anas americana*.

will-o'-the-wisp, colloquial name for the Common Nighthawk, *Chordeiles minor*.

wildfowl, British term for quarry species (other than gallinaceous game birds), including ducks, geese, and shorebirds.

windhover, colloquial name for the American Kestrel (sparrow hawk), *Falco sparverius*.

window-fighting, *n.*, a practice by territorial birds, particularly males, of fighting reflections in windows, mirrors, hubcaps, etc.

wings, *n.*, paired, feathered, lateral protuberances from the sides of the torso, containing a number of adapted and fused bones, used for flight, swimming underwater, courtship, noise-making, self-defense, and other purposes; see also Campbell & Lack, pp. 654-7.

wing bar, *n.*, distinctive coloration of the tertiary or secondary wing coverts, appearing as a bar across the wing; **[field mark]**.

wing coverts, *n.*, the smaller feathers overlying the bases of the wing flight feathers (remiges), named for the covered flight feathers (for example, the primary coverts overlie the primary flight feathers). Sections of feathers on the wing. The lesser wing coverts form a defined tract anterior to the middle coverts and back to the anterior border of the inner wing; the median or middle coverts, usually in a single row, are situated between the lesser and greater wing coverts. Middle coverts usually overlap one another in the reverse manner from the other coverts. The under-primary coverts are the feathers on the undersurface of the wing; **[field mark]**. *See illustration, p. 148.*

wing lining, *n.*, soft feathers on the under surface of the wing, including the lesser and median wing coverts.

winnowing, *n.*, roaring sound made by snipe diving and then pulling sharply out of the dive, often associated with mating and territorial displays.

winter chippy, colloquial name for the American Tree Sparrow, *Spizella arborea*.

wire-tail, colloquial name for the Ruddy Duck, *Oxyura jamaicensis*.

wishbone, *n.*, the Y-shaped breastbone made of the fused clavicles; also called the **furcula**.

woodcock, substantive name for the American Woodcock, *Scolopax minor*, or the Eurasian Woodcock, *Scolopax rusticola*.

woodpecker, family and substantive name of most species of the family *Picidae*, insectivorous, small and medium-sized birds

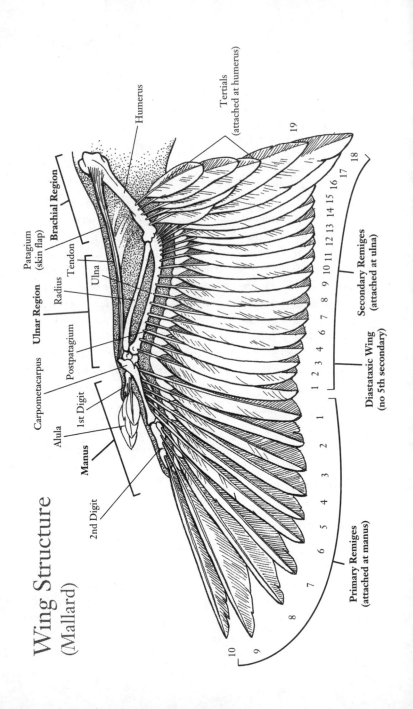

Wing Structure
(Mallard)

Humerus

Tertials
(attached at humerus)

Brachial Region

Patagium
(skin flap)

Tendon

Radius

Ulnar Region

Ulna

Carpometacarpus

Postpatagium

Alula

Manus

1st Digit

2nd Digit

Secondary Remiges
(attached at ulna)

Diastataxic Wing
(no 5th secondary)

Primary Remiges
(attached at manus)

1 2 3 4 5 6 7 8 9 10

1 2 3 4 5 6 7 8 9 10 11 12 13 14 15 16 17 18 19

with stiff tails and specially adapted skulls and tongues; see also Terres, pp. 1013-26.

wood-warblers, members of the subfamily *Parulinae*, family *Emberizidae*, consisting of sixteen North American genera comprising approximately forty-eight species; small, often brightly marked insectivorous birds with slender bills that are active, restless singers.

wren, family and substantive name for the members of the family *Troglodytidae*, which includes nine North American species. Wrens are small, erect-tailed, noisy, active birds with fine streaking and barring; see also Terres, pp. 1027-48.

wrist, *n.*, the portion of the leading edge of the wing where the forearm joins the manus (fused bones of the "hand"). The wrist joint joins the radius and ulna to the carpals.

Xx

xanthochroism, *n.*, an abnormal yellowing of the plumage caused by loss of dark pigment, allowing lighter pigments to dominate; rare in the wild but common among captives.

xerophilus, *adj.*, describing something adapted to living in a dry climate.

xiphoid, *adj.*, sword-shaped.

Yy

yellowbird, colloquial name for the American Goldfinch, *Carduelis tristis*, or the Yellow Warbler, *Dendroica petechia*.

yellow-hammer, colloquial name for the Yellow-shafted race of the Northern Flicker, *Colaptes auratus*.

yellowlegs, substantive name for two species of sandpipers, *Tringa* spp.

yellow-nose, colloquial name for the Black Scoter, *Melanitta nigra*.

yellowshanks, see **yellowlegs**.

yellowthroat, substantive name for *Geothlypis trichas*, a wood-warbler.

yelper, colloquial name for the American Avocet, *Recurvirostra americana*, Greater Yellowlegs, *Tringa melanoleuca*, and the cackling race of the Canada Goose, *Branta canadensis minima*.

yucker, colloquial name for the Northern Flicker, *Colaptes auritus*.

Zz

zone, *n.*, a broad band of color encircling the body; compare to **band**, **bar**, **belt**.

zoogeography, *n.*, the study of the distribution, movement, migration, range expansion, and ecology of living organisms, with reference to habitat types and range characteristics.

zoology, *n.*, the scientific study of animals; one branch, the study of birds, is **ornithology**.

zygodactyl, *adj.*, yoke-toed, describing feet with the first and fourth toes pointing to the rear and the second and third toes pointing to the front (for example, the feet of woodpeckers, owls, osprey, and parrots); see also **foot**. *See illustration, p. 62.*

zygomatic arch, *n.*, facial bones; same as **zygomatic bars**.

zygomatic bars, *n.*, facial bones, specifically the delicate rods that connect the quadrates with the bones composing the base of the upper mandible. *See illustration, p. 125.*

BIBLIOGRAPHY

American Ornithologists' Union (AOU). 1983. *Check-list of North American Birds*, 6th ed. Lawrence, Kans.: American Ornithologists' Union.

Bellrose, Frank C. 1976. *Ducks, Geese, and Swans of North America*. Harrisburg, Penn.: Stackpole Books. A new and expanded version of the important compilation made by F. H. Kortwright in 1942, with thorough color illustrations of waterfowl plumage variations and much detail about migration, plumage, nesting, and behavior.

Bent, Arthur Cleveland, ed. 1937. *Life Histories of American Birds*. 18 vols. New York: Dover Publications. Originally published by the Smithsonian Institution, this massive collection is made up of field observations by hundreds of scientists and volunteers regarding behavior, nests, eggs, migration, predation, songs—everything about birds that can be seen, heard, or measured.

Campbell, Bruce, and Elizabeth Lack, eds. 1985. *A Dictionary of Birds*. Vermillion, S. Dak.: Buteo Books. An excellent 670-page encyclopedia of ornithology, sponsored by the British Ornithologists' Union; also published in Britain by Poyser (Calton). The book is an updated and slightly condensed revision of Thomson's 1964 *A New Dictionary of Birds*, now out of print.

Choate, Ernest A. 1985. *The Dictionary of American Bird Names*, Rev. ed. Boston: The Harvard Common Press. A complete and accurate compendium of common and scientific names of all bird species of North America, with historical information regarding prominent ornithologists after whom many species have been named. Latin/English glossary helps readers understand the meanings of scientific names. 226 pp.

Ehrlich, Paul R., D. S. Dobkin, and D. Wheye. 1988. *The Birder's Handbook*. New York: Simon & Schuster. Fact-packed supplemental natural history of all North American birds, with copious notes on diet, habitat, nesting habits, and behavior; indispensable, as advertised, "The Essential Companion to Your Identification Guide."

Fisher, James, and Roger Tory Peterson. 1964. *The World of Birds*. New York: Doubleday. Thorough explanation of all facets of ornithology in terms easily understood by the layman. Includes many of Peterson's illustrations, topped off with world maps showing distribution of all suborders, lists of extinct and endangered species, and an extensive bibliography. 288 pp.

Halliday, Tim. 1978. *Vanishing Birds: Their Natural History and Conservation*. New York: Holt, Rinehart & Winston. 296 pp.

McEneaney, Terry. 1993. *The Birder's Guide to Montana*. Helena, Mont.: Falcon Press. Of the many state birding guides out there, this is one of the best. McEneaney's service as a wildlife biologist at Red Rock Lakes National Wildlife Refuge and Yellowstone National Park and his daily work with birders and ornithologists all over Montana contribute to the text.

Monroe, Burt L., Jr., and Charles G. Sibley. 1990. *Distribution and Taxonomy of Birds of the World*. New Haven, Conn.: Yale University Press. Called the most important text on avian taxonomy of the century, this book comes with an essential 1993 supplement. Monroe is the chairman of the AOU *Checklist* committee and a past AOU president. Sibley is professor emeritus of biology and ornithology at Yale University and another past president of the AOU. Their revolutionary reworking of bird relationships relies heavily upon modern DNA analyses.

Monroe, Burt L., Jr., and Charles G. Sibley. *A World Checklist of Birds*. 1993. New Haven, Conn.: Yale University Press. This list of 9,702 species of birds is organized in accordance with Sibley and Ahlquist's *Phylogeny and Classification of Birds* (1990). This list is nothing more, and nothing less, than a complete species checklist organized by subclass, infraorder, and so forth, based on the gene studies of Sibley, Ahlquist, Monroe, and other workers who have revolutionized avian systematics.

National Geographic Society. 1987. *Field Guide to the Birds of North America*. Washington D.C.: National Geographic Society. No-nonsense, well-illustrated, easy-to-use field guide organized in accord with the 1983 AOU *Check-list*, with range maps. One of the author's favorites.

Pettingill, Owen S., Jr. *Ornithology in Laboratory and Field*, 4th ed. Minneapolis, Minn.: Burgess Publishing. 524 pp.

Proctor, Noble S., and Patrick J. Lynch. 1993. *Manual of Ornithology*. New Haven, Conn.: Yale University Press. Superlatives fail to adequately describe this state-of-the-art, marvelously illustrated reference work emphasizing form and function more than behavior. It contains fresh and thoroughly documented discussions of both evolution and systematics.

Queeny, Edgar M. 1947. *Prairie Wings: The Classic Illustrated Study of American Wildfowl in Flight*, Reprint. New York: Dover Publications. It lives up to its name.

Robbins, Chandler S., B. Bruun, H. S. Zim, and A. Singer. 1983. *Birds of North America*, Rev. ed. New York: Golden Press. Organized, compact, well-illustrated, easy-to-use field guide, generally arranged in accord with the 1983 AOU *Check-list*, with range maps and "sonagrams" of songs. This is the author's other favorite field guide.

Ruppell, Georg. 1977. *Bird Flight*, Reprint. New York: Van Nostrand Reinhold. Originally published in Germany in 1975 as Vogelflug. Excellent photos and explanations of the physics and mechanics of avian flight.

Ryser, Fred A., Jr. 1985. *Birds of the Great Basin: A Natural History*. Reno, Nev.: University of Nevada Press. Exquisitely detailed and heavily endnoted, a tour de force on the environment and ecology of the Great Basin and the birds that inhabit it. Includes many excellent photos, (although illustration is not its strong point) and descriptions of behavior.

Sibley, Charles G., and J.E. Ahlquist. 1990. *Phylogeny and Classification of Birds*. New Haven, Conn.: Yale University Press.

Terres, John K. 1980. *The Audubon Society Encyclopedia of North American Birds*. New York: Alfred A. Knopf. An essential reference work that should be in every public library. Comprehensive if uniquely organized, superbly illustrated with photos and drawings, this book includes thorough and well-documented explanations of breeding, nesting, migration, diets, behavior, habits, families, evolution—in short, everything one needs to know about birds.

Thayer, Gerald H. 1909. *Concealing Coloration in the Animal Kingdom*. New York: The MacMillan Co.

Thomson, A. Landsborough. 1964. *A New Dictionary of Birds*. New York: McGraw-Hill. Copyrighted by the British Ornithologists' Union in celebration of its centenary and in honor of Professor Alfred Newton's *A Dictionary of Birds* (1896), with classification based loosely upon the *Check-list of Birds of the World*. This classic version has illustrations that are adequate but not remarkable and text that is thorough, well documented, and cross-referenced. See also Campbell and Lack's excellent updated version.

Whitney, Stephen, ed. 1985. *Western Forests: A National Audubon Society Nature Guide*. New York: Alfred A. Knopf. If you must carry one field guide for flowers, trees, birds, mammals, reptiles, and general ecology, this Audubon Society Nature Guide is an excellent choice. *Grasslands* (1985; Lauren Brown, ed.) is another fine member of the series.

APPENDIX I
NORTH AMERICAN FAMILIES (ALPHABETICAL)

See Appendix II, Orders, for a systematic taxonomic listing; this alphabetical listing is provided for readers not familiar with systematic taxonomy.

Accipitridae, hawks, falcons, and eagles

Alaudidae, larks

Alcedinidae, kingfishers

Alcidae, puffins, auks, and murres

Anatidae, ducks, geese, and swans

Apodidae, swifts

Aramidae, limpkin

Ardeidae, herons and bitterns

Bombycillidae, waxwings

Caprimulgidae, nighthawks and poor-wills

Cathartidae, vultures

Certhiidae, creepers

Chamaeidae, wrentits

Charadriidae, plovers

Ciconiidae, storks

Cinclidae, dippers

Columbidae, doves and pigeons

Corvidae, crows, jays, and magpies

Cotingidae, cotingas

Cuculidae, cuckoos, roadrunners, and anis

Diomedeidae, albatrosses

Falconidae, falcons and caracaras

Fregatidae, frigatebirds

Fringillidae, finches, grosbeaks, buntings, and sparrows

Gaviidae, loons

Gruidae, cranes

Haematopodidae, oystercatchers

Hirundinidae, swallows

Hydrobatidae, storm petrels

Icteridae, blackbirds, meadowlarks, and orioles

Laniidae, shrikes

Laridae, gulls and terns

Meleagridae, turkeys

Mimidae, mockingbirds and thrashers

Motacillidae, pipits and wagtails

Pandionidae, osprey

Paridae, titmice, verdins, chickadees, and bushtits

Parulidae, wood warblers

Pelecanidae, pelicans

Phaetontidae, tropicbirds

Phalacrocoracidae, cormorants

Phalaropodidae, phalaropes

Phasianidae, pheasants, partridges, and quail

Picidae, woodpeckers

Ploceidae, weavers and Old World finches

Podicipedidae, grebes

Procellariidae, shearwaters, fulmars, and petrels

Ptilogonatidae, silky flycatchers

Rallidae, rails, gallinules, and coots

Recurvirostridae, avocets and stilts

Scolopacidae, woodcocks, snipe, and sandpipers

Sittidae, nuthatches

Stercorariidae, jaegers and skuas

Strigidae, owls

Sturnidae, starlings

Sulidae, boobies and gannets

Sylviidae, kinglets, gnatcatchers, and Old World warblers

Tetraonidae, grouse and ptarmigan

Thraupidae, tanagers

Threskiornithidae, ibises and spoonbills

Trochilidae, hummingbirds

Troglodytidae, wrens

Trogonidae, trogons

Turdidae, robins, bluebirds, solitaires, and thrushes

Tyrannidae, tyrant flycatchers

Tytonidae, barn owls

Vireonidae, vireos

APPENDIX II
NORTH AMERICAN ORDERS

The following orders, listed systematically by North American families, are included in the American Ornithological Union's *Check-list*, 6th ed., 1983.

Gaviiformes, loons
    Gaviidae, loon family
Podicipediformes, grebes
    Podicipedidae, grebe family
Procellariiformes, albatrosses, fulmars, petrels
    Diomedeidae, albatross family
    Procellariidae, fulmar and petrel family
    Hydrobatidae, storm-petrel family
Pelicaniformes, pelicans, gannets, cormorants, anhingas
    Phaethontidae, tropicbird family
    Sulidae, gannet and booby family
    Pelecanidae, pelican family
    Phalacrocoracidae, cormorant family
    Anhingidae, anhinga family
    Fregatidae, frigatebird family
Ciconiiformes, herons, bitterns, ibises, storks, spoonbills
    Ardeidae, heron and bittern family
    Threskiornithidae, ibis and spoonbill family
    Ciconiidae, stork family
Phoenicopteriformes, flamingos
    Phoenicopteridae, flamingos
Anseriformes, geese, ducks, swans
  Anseres, waterfowl suborder
    Anatidae, geese, ducks, swans family
      Anserinae, whistling-duck, geese, swan subfamily
        Cygnini, swans (tribe)
        Anserini, geese (tribe)

        Dendrocygnini, whistling-ducks (tribe)

      Anatinae, duck subfamily

        Anatini, marsh ducks (tribe)

        Cairinini, wood duck (tribe)

        Aythyini, bay ducks (tribe)

        Mergini, mergansers, eiders, sea ducks (tribe)

        Oxyurini, stiff-tailed ducks (tribe)

Falconiformes, vultures, hawks, eagles, ospreys

  Cathartidae, vulture family

  Accipitridae, hawk family

    Accipitrinae, kite, hawk, eagle subfamily

    Pandioninae, osprey subfamily

  Falconidae, falcon, caracara family

    Falconini, falcons (tribe)

    Polyborini, caracaras (tribe)

Galliformes, partridges, grouse, turkeys, chachalacas

  Cracidae, chachalaca family

  Phasianidae, partridge, pheasant family

    Phasianinae, pheasant subfamily

    Tetraoninae, grouse, ptarmigan subfamily

    Meleagridinae, turkey subfamily

    Odontophorinae, quail subfamily

Gruiformes, cranes, rails, limpkins, coots, gallinules

  Rallidae, rail, coot, gallinule family

  Aramidae, limpkin family

  Gruidae, crane family

Charadriiformes, plovers, stilts, sandpipers, gulls, terns

  Charadriidae, plover family

  Haematopodidae, oystercatcher family

  Recurvirostridae, stilt, avocet family

  Jacanidae, jacana family

  Scolopacidae, sandpiper, phalarope family

  Laridae, gull, tern, skimmer family

    Larinae, gull subfamily

    Stercorariinae, jaeger, skua subfamily

Sterninae, tern subfamily

Rynchopinae, skimmer subfamily

Alcidae, auk, murre, auklet, puffin, guillemot family

Columbiformes, pigeons, doves

Columbidae, pigeon, dove family

Psittaciformes, parrots

Psittacidae, parrot family

Cuculiformes, roadrunners, cuckoos, anis

Cuculidae, roadrunner, cuckoo family

Strigiformes, owls

Tytonidae, barn owl family

Strigidae, owl family

Caprimulgiformes, nighthawks, poor-wills

Caprimulgidae, nighthawk, poor-will family

Apodiformes, swifts, hummingbirds

Apodidae, swift family

Trochilidae, hummingbird family

Trogoniformes, trogons

Trogonidae, trogon family

Coraciiformes, kingfishers

Alcedinidae, kingfisher family

Piciformes, woodpeckers

Picidae, woodpecker family

Passeriformes, perching birds

Tyrannidae, flycatcher family

Alaudidae, lark family

Motacillidae, pipit family

Hirundinidae, swallow family

Corvidae, crow, raven, jay family

Paridae, chickadee, titmice family

Remizidae, verdin family

Aegithalidae, bushtit family

Sittidae, nuthatch family

Certhiidae, creeper family

Troglodytidae, wren family

Pycnonotidae, bulbul family

Cinclidae, dipper family

Muscicapidae, kinglet, gnatcatcher, thrush family

    Sylviinae, warbler, kinglet, gnatcatcher subfamily

    Muscicapinae, Old World flycatcher subfamily

    Turdinae, bluebird, solitaire, thrush subfamily

    Timaliinae, wrentit subfamily

Mimidae, thrasher (mimic thrush) family

Laniidae, shrike family

Sturnidae, starling family

Bombycillidae, waxwing family

Ptilogonatidae, silky flycatcher family

Vireonidae, vireo family

Emberizidae, emberizid family

    Parulinae, wood warbler subfamily

    Icterinae, oriole, blackbird subfamily

    Thraupinae, tanager subfamily

    Emberizinae, sparrow, junco, towhee subfamily

    Cardinalinae, grosbeak, bunting subfamily

Fringillidae, finch family

Ploceidae, weaver finch family

Passeridae, Old World sparrow family

APPENDIX III
WORLD ORDERS

The following world orders are listed systematically, in accord with traditional nomenclature, and do not include extinct orders and families. See *The World of Birds*, Fisher and Peterson, 1964.

Sphenisciformes, penguins
    Spheniscidae, penguin family
Struthioniformes, ostriches
    Struthionidae, ostrich family
Casuariiformes, emus and cassowaries
    Dromiceiidae, emu family
    Casuariidae, cassowary family
Apterygiformes, moas and kiwis
   Apteryges, kiwi suborder
    Apterygidae, kiwi family
Rheiformes, rheas
    Rheidae, rhea family
Tinamiformes, tinamous
    Tinamidae, tinamou family
Gaviiformes, loons
    Gaviidae, loon family
Podicipediformes, grebes
    Podicipedidae, grebe family
Procellariiformes, albatrosses and petrels
    Diomedeidae, albatross family
    Procellariidae, petrel and shearwater family
    Oceanitidae, storm-petrel family
    Pelecanoididae, diving petrel family
Pelecaniformes, pelicans and tropicbirds
   Phaethontes, tropicbird suborder
    Phaethontidae, tropicbird family

Pelecani, pelican suborder

    Pelicanidae, pelican family

Sulae, gannet suborder

    Sulidae, gannet and booby family

    Phalacrocoracidae, cormorant family

    Anhingidae, anhinga family

Fregatae, frigatebird suborder

    Fregatidae, frigatebird family

Ciconiiformes, storks, herons, and ibises

  Ardeae, heron suborder

    Ardeidae, heron family

  Ciconiae, stork suborder

    Scopidae, hammerhead family

    Ciconiidae, stork family

    Balaenicipitidae, shoebill family

  Plataleae, ibis and spoonbill suborder

    Plataleidae, ibis and spoonbill family

Phoenicopteriformes, flamingos

    Phoenicopteridae, flamingo family

Anseriformes, geese, ducks, and swans

  Anhimae, screamer suborder

    Anhimidae, screamer family

  Anseres, waterfowl suborder

Falconiformes, birds of prey

  Cathartae, vulture suborder

    Cathartidae, New World vulture family

  Falcones, hawk and eagle suborder

    Sagittariidae, secretary bird family

    Accipitridae, hawk and eagle family

    Pandionidae, osprey family

    Falconidae, falcon family

Galliformes, grouse and quail

  Opisthocomi, hoatzin suborder

    Opisthocomidae, hoatzin family

  Galli, grouse and guinea fowl suborder

Cracidae, guan and curassow family

Megapodiidae, megapode family

Tetraonidae, grouse family

Phasianidae, pheasant family

Numididae, guinea fowl family

Meleagrididae, turkey family

Gruiformes, cranes, Madagascan roatelos, limpkins, rails

Mesoanides or mesoenatides, Madagascan roatelos suborder

Mesoenatidae, Madagascan roatelos family

Turnices, Old World quail suborder

Turnicidae, bustard quail family

Pedionomidae, plains wanderer family

Grues, crane suborder

Gruidae, crane family

Aramidae, limpkin family

Psophiidae, trumpeter family

Rallidae, rail family

Heliornithes, finfoot suborder

Heliornithidae, finfoot family

Rhynocheti, kagu suborder

Rhynochetidae, kagu family

Eurypygae, sun bittern suborder

Eurypygidae, sun bittern family

Cariamae, seriemas suborder

Cariamidae, seriemas family

Otides, bustard suborder

Otididae, bustard family

Charadriiformes, shorebirds

Charadrii, plover, snipe, avocet suborder

Jacanidae, jacana family

Rostratulidae, painted snipe family

Haematopodidae, oystercatcher family

Charadriidae, plover family

Scolopacidae, sandpiper family

Recurvirostridae, avocet family

Phalaropodidae, phalarope family

Dromadidae, crab plover family

Burhinidae, thick-knee family

Glareolidae, courser family

Thinocoridae, seed snipe family

Chionididae, sheathbill family

Lari, gulls, terns, and skua suborder

Stercorariidae, skua family

Laridae, gull and tern family

Rynchopidae, skimmer family

Alcae, auk suborder

Alcidae, auk family

Columbiformes, pigeons and doves

Pterocletes, sand grouse suborder

Pteroclidae, sand grouse family

Columbae, dove and pigeon suborder

Columbidae, pigeon and dove family

Psittaciformes, parrots

Psittacidae, parrot family

Musophagiformes, touracos

Musophagidae, touraco family

Cuculiformes, cuckoos

Cuculidae, cuckoo family

Strigiformes, owls

Tytonidae, barn owl family

Strigidae, typical owl family

Caprimulgiformes, frogmouths, nightjars, and nighthawks

Steatornithes, oilbird suborder

Steatornithidae, oilbird family

Caprimulgi, frogmouth and nighthawk suborder

Aegothelidae, owlet frogmouth family

Podargidae, frogmouth family

Caprimulgidae, nightjar and nighthawk family

Nyctibiidae, potoo family

Apodiformes, swifts and hummingbirds

Apodi, swift suborder

    Apodidae, swift family

  Trochili, hummingbird suborder

    Trochilidae, hummingbird family

Coliiformes, colies

    Coliidae, colies family

Trogoniformes, trogons

    Trogonidae, trogon family

Coraciiformes, kingfishers

  Alcedines, kingfisher suborder

    Alcedinidae, kingfisher family

    Todidae, tody family

    Momotidae, motmot family

  Meropes, bee eater suborder

    Meropidae, bee eater family

  Coracii, roller and hoopoe suborder

    Coraciidae, roller family

    Brachypteraciidae, ground roller family

    Leptosomatidae, cuckoo roller family

    Upupidae, hoopoe family

    Phoeniculidae, wood hoopoe family

  Bucerotes, hornbill suborder

    Bucerotidae, hornbill family

Piciformes, woodpeckers, barbets, and toucans

  Galbulae, barbet suborder

    Galbulidae, jacamar family

    Bucconidae, puffbird family

    Capitonidae, barbet family

    Indicatoridae, honeyguide family

    Ramphastidae, toucan family

  Pici, woodpecker suborder

    Picidae, woodpecker family

Passeriformes, perching birds

  Eurylaimi, broadbill suborder

    Eurylaimidae, broadbill family

Tyranni, flycatcher, pitta, ovenbird suborder

   Furnariidae, woodhewer and ovenbird family

    Dendrocolaptinae, woodhewer subfamily

    Furnariinae, ovenbird subfamily

   Formicariidae, ant thrush family

   Conopophagidae, ant pipit family

   Rhinocryptidae, tapaculo family

   Pittidae, pitta family

   Philepittidae, asities family

   Acanthisittidae, New Zealand wren family

   Tyrannidae, tyrant flycatcher family

   Pipridae, manakin family

   Cotingidae, cotinga family

   Phytotomidae, plantcutter family

Menurae, lyrebird suborder

   Menuridae, lyrebird family

   Atrichornithidae, scrub bird family

Passeres, passerine (singing birds) suborder

   Alaudidae, lark family

   Hirundinidae, swallow family

   Motacillidae, wagtail and pipit family

   Campephagidae, cuckoo shrike family

   Pycnonotidae, bulbul family

   Irenidae, leaf bird family

   Laniidae, shrike family

   Vangidae, vanga shrike family

   Bombycillidae, waxwing family

   Dulidae, palm chat family

   Cinclidae, dipper family

   Troglodytidae, wren family

   Mimidae, thrasher and mockingbird family

   Prunellidae, accentor family

   Muscicapidae, thrush family

    Turdinae, thrush subfamily

    Timaliinae, babbler subfamily

Panurinae, bearded tit and parrotbill subfamily

Polioptilinae, gnatcatcher subfamily

Sylviinae, Old World warbler subfamily

Malurinae, Australian warbler subfamily

Muscicapinae, Old World flycatcher subfamily

Monarchinae, monarch subfamily

Pachycephalinae, whistler subfamily

Picathartinae, bald crow subfamily

Paridae, titmouse family

Sittidae, nuthatch family

Certhiidae, creeper family

Dicacidae, flowerpecker family

Nectariniidae, sunbird family

Zosteropidae, whiteye family

Meliphagidae, honeyeater family

Emberizidae, warbler, oriole, and sparrow family

   Emberizinae, bunting and American sparrow subfamily

   Cardinalinae, cardinal subfamily

   Catamblyrhynchinae, plush-capped finch subfamily

   Tanagrinae, tanager subfamily

   Tersininae, swallow tanager subfamily

   Coerebinae, honeycreeper subfamily

Parulidae, wood warbler family

Drepanididae, Hawaiian honeycreeper family

Vireonidae, vireo family

Icteridae, blackbird and oriole family

Fringillidae, finch family

Estrildidae, waxbill family

Viduidae, widow bird family

Ploceidae, weaver and true sparrow family

Sturnidae, starling family

Oriolidae, Old World oriole family

Dicruridae, drongo family

Callaeidae, wattled crow family

Grallinidae, magpie lark family

Artamidae, wood swallow family
Cracticidae, bell magpie family
Ptilonorhynchidae, bower bird family
Paradisaeidae, bird of paradise family
Corvidae, crow family

APPENDIX IV
SIBLEY - AHLQUIST - MONROE (SAM) CLASSIFICATION SYSTEM OF WORLD ORDERS

The following group affinities are based on DNA data as described in research by Monroe, Sibley, and Ahlquist 1985, 1990. The following categorization follows the 1993 *Manual of Ornithology*. See the bibliography for full citations.

CLASS AVES

Subclass **Neornithes** (2,057 genera/9,672 species)[1]

Infraclass **Eoaves** (14 genera/57 species)

Parvclass Ratitae

    ORDER **STRUTHIONIFORMES** (5 genera/10 species)

      Suborder **Struthioni**

       Infraorder **Struthionides**

          Family **Struthionidae** (1/1) - ostrich

       Infraorder **Rheides**

          Family **Rheidae** (1/2) - rheas

      Suborder **Casuarii**

          Family **Casuariidae** (2/4)

            Tribe **Casuariini** - cassowaries

            Tribe **Dromaiini** - emu

          Family **Apterygidae** (1/3) - kiwis

    ORDER **TINAMIFORMES** (9 genera/47 species)

          Family **Tinamidae** (9/47) - tinamous

Infraclass **Neoaves** (2,043 genera/9,615 species)

Parvclass Galloanserae

    Superorder **Gallomorphae**

---

[1] Burt Monroe and Charles Sibley, *A World Checklist of Birds* (Yale University Press, 1983) list 2,063 genera and 9,702 species in this subclass. The subclass **Neornithes** refers to geologically recent species, distinguished from species found only in the fossil record.

ORDER **CRACIFORMES** (17 genera/ 69 species)

  Suborder **Craci**

        Family **Cracidae** (11/50) - guans, chachalacas, curassows

  Suborder **Megapodii**

        Family **Megapodiidae** (6/19) - megapodes

ORDER **GALLIFORMES** (58 genera/2l4 species)

    Parvorder **Phasianida**

      Superfamily **Phasianoidea**

        Family **Phasianidae** (45/177) - pheasants, grouse, turkeys, partridges

      Superfamily **Numidoidea**

        Family **Numididae** (4/6) - guineafowls

    Parvorder **Odontophorida**

        Family **Odontophoridae** (4/6) - New World quail

  Superorder **Anserimorphae**

ORDER **ANSERIFORMES** (48 genera/161 species)

    Infraorder **Anhimides**

      Superfamily **Anhimoidea**

        Family **Anhimidae** (2/3) - screamers

      Superfamily **Anseranatoidea**

        Family **Anseranatidae** (1/1) - magpie goose

    Infraorder **Anserides**

        Family **Dendrocygnidae** (2/9) - whistling-ducks

        Family **Anatidae** (43/148)

          Subfamily **Oxyurinae** - stiff-tailed ducks

          Subfamily **Stictonettinae** - Stictonetta

          Subfamily **Cygninae** - swans

          Subfamily **Anatinae** - typical ducks, geese

Parvclass Turnicae

  ORDER TURNICIFORMES (2 genera/17 species)

      Family **Turnicidae** - buttonquails

Parvclass Picae

  ORDER **PICIFORMES** (51 genera/355 species)

    Infraorder **Picides**

Family **Indicatoridae** (4/17) - honeyguides

Family **Picidae** (28/215) - woodpeckers, wrynecks, piculets

Infraorder **Ramphastides**

Superfamily **Megalaimoidea**

Family **Megalaimoidae** (3/26) - Asian barbets

Superfamily **Lybioidea**

Family **Lybiidae** (7/42) - African barbets

Superfamily **Ramphastoidea**

Family **Rhamphastidae** (9/55)

Subfamily **Capitoninae** - New World barbets

Subfamily **Ramphastinae** - toucans

Parvclass Coraciae

Superorder **Galbulimorphae**

ORDER **GALBULIFORMES** (15 genera/51 species)

Infraorder **Galbulides**

Family **Galbulidae** (5/18) - jacamars

Infraorder **Bucconides**

Family **Bucconidae** (10/33) - puff birds

Superorder **Bucerotimonphae**

ORDER **BUCEROTIFORMES** (9 genera/56 species)

Family **Bucerotidae** (8/54) - typical hornbills

Family **Bucorvidae** (1/2) - ground-hornbills

ORDER **UPUPIFORMES** (3 genera/10 species)

Infraorder **Upupides**

Family **Upupidae** (1/2) - hoopoes

Infraorder **Phoeniculides**

Family **Phoeniculidae** (1/5) - wood hoopoes

Family **Rhinopomastidae** (1/3) - scimitarbills

Superorder **Coraciimorphae**

ORDER **TROGONIFORMES** (6 genera/39 species)

Family **Trogonidae** (6/39)

Subfamily **Apaloderminae** - African trogons

Subfamily **Trogoninae**

Tribe **Trogonini** - New World trogons

Tribe **Harpactini** - Asian trogons

ORDER **CORACIIFORMES** (34 genera /152 species)

Suborder **Coracii**

Superfamily **Coracioidea**

Family **Coraciidae** (2/12) - typical rollers

Family **Brachypteraciidae** (3/5) - ground-rollers

Superfamily **Leptosomoidea**

Family **Leptosomidae** (1/1) - cuckoo-roller

Suborder **Alcedini**

Infraorder **Alcedinides**

Parvorder **Momotida**

Family **Momotidae** (6/9) - motmots

Parvorder **Todida**

Family **Todidae** (1/5) - todies

Parvorder **Alcedinida**

Family **Alcedinidae** (3/24) - Alcedinid kingfishers

Parvorder **Cerylida**

Superfamily **Dacelonoidea**

Family **Dacelonidae** (12/61) - Dacelonid kingfishers

Superfamily **Ceryloidea**

Family **Cerylidae** (3/9) - Cerylid kingfishers

Infraorder **Meropides**

Family **Meropidae** (3/26) - bee-eaters

Parvclass Coliae

ORDER **COLIIFORMES** (2 genera/6 species)

Family **Coliidae** (2/6)

Subfamily **Coliinae** - typical mousebirds

Subfamily **Urocoliinae** - long-tailed mousebirds

Parvclass Passerae

Superorder **Cuculimorphae**

ORDER **CUCULIFORMES** (30 genera/143 species)

Infraorder **Cuculides**

Parvorder **Cuculida**

  Superfamily **Cuculoidea**

    Family **Cuculidae** (17/79) - Old World cuckoos

  Superfamily **Centropodoidea**

    Family **Centropodidae** (1/30) - **Coucals**

  Superfamily **Coccyzida**

    Family **Coccyzidae** (4/18) - American cuckoos

Infraorder **Crotophagides**

Parvorder **Opisthocomida**

    Family **Opisthocomidae** (1/1) - hoatzin

Parvorder **Crotophagida**

    Family **Crotophagidae** (2/4)

      Tribe **Crotophagini** - anis

      Tribe **Guirini** - Guira cuckoo

Parvorder **Neomorphida**

    Family **Neomorphidae** (5/11) - roadrunners, ground-cuckoos

Superorder **Psittacimorphae**

ORDER **PSITTACIFORMES** (80 genera/358 species)

    Family **Psittacidae** (5/17) - parrots and allies

Superorder **Apodimorphae**

ORDER **APODIFORMES** (19 genera/103 species)

    Family **Apodidae** (18/99) - typical swifts

    Family **Hemiprocnidae** (1/4) - crested swifts

ORDER **TROCHILIFORMES** (709 genera/319 species)

    Family **Trochilidae** (709/319)

      Subfamily **Phaethornithinae** - hermits

      Subfamily **Trochilinae** - typical hummingbirds

Superorder **Strigimorphae**

ORDER **MUSOPHAGIFORMES** (5 genera/23 species)

    Family **Musophagidae** (5/23)

      Subfamily **Musophaginae** - turacos

      Subfamily **Criniferinae** - plantain-eaters

ORDER **STRIGIFORMES** (45 genera/291 species)

  Suborder **Strigi**

    Parvorder **Tytonida**

Family **Tytonidae** (2/17) - barn owl, grass owls

Parvorder **Strigida**

Family **Strigidae** (23/161) - tropical owls

Suborder **Aegotheli**

Family **Aegothelidae** (1/8) - owlet-nightjars

Suborder **Caprimulgi**

Infraorder **Podargides**

Family **Podargidae** (1 /3) - Australian frogmouths

Family **Batrachostomidae** (1/11) - Asian frogmouths

Infraorder **Caprimulgides**

Parvorder **Steatornithida**

Superfamily **Steatornithoidea**

Family **Steatornithidae** (1/1) - oilbird

Superfamily **Nyctibioidea**

Family **Nyctibiidae** (1/7) - potoos

Parvorder **Caprimulgida**

Superfamily **Eurostopodoidea**

Family **Eurostopodidae** (1/7) - eared-nightjars

Superfamily **Caprimulgoidea**

Family **Caprimulgidae** (14/76)

Subfamily **Chordeilinae** - nighthawks

Subfamily **Caprimulginae** - nightjars

Superorder **Passerimorphae**

ORDER **COLUMBIFORMES** (42 genera/313 species)

Family **Raphidae** (2/3) - dodos, solitaires (extinct)

Family **Columbidae** (40/310) - pigeons, doves

ORDER **GRUIFORMES** (53 genera/196 species)

Suborder **Grui**

Infraorder **Eurypygidoes**

Family **Eurypygidae** (1/1) - sun bittern

Infraorder **Otidides**

Family **Otididae** (6/25) - bustards

Infraorder **Gruides**

Parvorder **Gruida**

Superfamily **Gruoidea**

Family **Gruidae** (2/15)

Subfamily **Balearicinae** - crowned-cranes

Subfamily **Gruinae** - typical cranes

Family **Heliornithidae** (4/4)

Tribe **Aramini** - limpkin

Tribe **Heliornithini** - sun grebes

Superfamily **Psophioidea**

Family **Psophiidae** (1/3) - trumpeters

Parvorder **Cariamida**

Family **Cariamidae** (2/?) - seriemas

Family **Rhynochetidae** (1/1) - kagu

Suborder **Ralli**

Family **Rallidae** (34/142) - rails, gallinules, coots

Suborder **Mesitornithi**

Family **Mesitornithidae** (2/3) - mesites, monias, roatelos

ORDER **CICONIIFORMES** (254 genera/1,027 species)

Suborder **Charadrii**

Infraorder **Pteroclides**

Family **Pteroclidae** (2/16) - sand grouse

Infraorder **Charadriides**

Parvorder **Scolopacida**

Superfamily **Scolopacoidea**

Family **Thinocoridae** (2/4) - seedsnipes

Family **Pedionomidae** (1/1) - Plains-wanderer

Family **Scolopacidae** (21/88)

Subfamily **Scolopacinae** - woodcocks, snipes

Subfamily **Tringinae** - sandpipers, curlews, phalaropes

Superfamily **Jacanoidea**

Family **Rostratulidae** (1/2) - painted snipe

Family **Jacanidae** (6/8) - jacanas, lily-trotters

Parvorder **Charadriida**

Superfamily **Chionidoidea**

Family **Chionididae** (1/2) - sheathbills

Superfamily **Charadrioidea**

Family **Burhinidae** (1/9) - thick-knees

179

Family **Charadriidae** (16/89)

  Subfamily **Recurvirostrinae**

    Tribe **Haematopodini** - oystercatchers

    Tribe **Recurvirostrini** - avocets, stilts

  Subfamily **Charadriinae** - plovers, lapwings

Superfamily **Laroidea**

  Family **Glareolidae** (6/18)

    Subfamily **Dromadinae** - crab-plover

    Subfamily **Glareolinae** - pratinicoles, coursers

  Family **Laridae** (28/129)

    Subfamily **Larinae**

      Tribe **Stercorariini** - skuas, jaegers

      Tribe **Rynchopini** - skimmers

      Tribe **Larini** - gulls

      Tribe **Sternini** - terns

    Subfamily **Alcinae** - auks, murres, puffins

Suborder **Ciconii**

Infraorder **Falconides**

Parvorder **Accipitrida**

  Family **Accipitridae** (65/240)

    Subfamily **Pandioninae** - osprey

    Subfamily **Accipitrinae** - hawks, eagles, accipiters, kites

  Family **Sagittariidae** (1/1) - secretary bird

Parvorder **Falconida**

  Family **Falconidae** (10/63) - falcons, caracaras

Infraorder **Ciconiides**

Parvorder **Podicipedida**

  Family **Podicipedidae** (6/21) - grebes

Parvorder **Phaethontida**

  Family **Phaethontidae** (1/3) - tropicbirds

Parvorder **Sulida**

  Superfamily **Suloidea**

    Family **Sulidae** (3/9) - boobies, gannets

    Family **Anhingidae** (1/4) - anhingas, darters

  Superfamily **Phalacrocoracoidea**

Family **Phalacrocoracidae** (1/38) - cormorants, shags

Parvorder **Ciconiida**

Superfamily **Ardeoidea**

Family **Ardeidae** (20/65) - herons, egrets, bitterns

Superfamily **Scopoidea**

Family **Scopidae** (l/1) - hamerkop (hammerhead)

Superfamily **Phoenicopteroidea**

Family **Phoenicopteridae** (1/5) - flamingos

Superfamily **Threskiornithoidea**

Family **Threskiornithidae** (14/34) - ibises, spoonbills

Superfamily **Pelecanoidea**

Family **Pelecanidae** (2/9)

Subfamily **Balaenicipitinae** - shoebill

Subfamily **Pelecaninae** - pelicans

Superfamily **Ciconioidea**

Family **Ciconiidae** (11/26)

Subfamily **Cathartinae** - New World vultures

Subfamily **Ciconiinae** - storks

Superfamily **Procellarioidea**

Family **Fregatidae** (1/5) - frigatebirds

Family **Spheniscidae** (6/17) - penguins

Family **Gaviidae** (1/5) - loons

Family **Procellariidae** (24/415)

Subfamily **Procellariinae** - petrels, shearwaters, diving-petrels

Subfamily **Diomedeinae** - albatrosses

Subfamily **Hydrobatinae** - storm-petrels

ORDER **PASSERIFORMES** (1,161 genera / 5,712 species)

Suborder **Tyranni** (Suboscines)

Infraorder **Acanthisittides**

Family **Acanthisittidae** (2/4) - New Zealand wrens

Infraorder **Eurylaimides**

Superfamily **Pittoidea**

Family **Pittidae** (1/31) - pittas

Superfamily **Eurylaimoidea**

Family **Eurylaimidae** (8/14) - broadbills

Family **Philepittidae** (2/4) - asities (asitys)

Infraorder/Family **Incertae sedos** (Sapayoa)

Infraorder **Tyrannides**

Parvorder **Tyrannida**

Family **Tyrannidae** (146/537)

Subfamily **Pipromorphinae** - Mionectine flycatchers, Corythopis

Subfamily **Tyranninae** - tyrant flycatchers

Subfamily **Tityrinae**

Tribe **Schiffornithini** - Schiffornis

Tribe **Tityrini** - tityras, becards

Subfamily **Cotinginae** - cotingas, plantcutters, sharpbill

Subfamily **Piprinae** - manakins

Parvorder **Thamnophilida**

Family **Thamnophilidae** (45/488) - typical antbirds

Parvorder **Furnariida**

Superfamily **Furnarioidea**

Family **Furnariidae** (66/280)

Subfamily **Furnariinae** - ovenbirds

Subfamily **Dendrocolaptinae** - woodcreepers

Superfamily **Formicarioidea**

Family **Formicariidae** (7/56) - ground antbirds

Family **Conopophagidae** (1/8) - gnateaters

Family **Rhinocryptidae** (12/28) - tapaculos

Suborder **Passeri** (Oscines)

Parvorder **Corvida**

Superfamily **Menuroidea**

Family **Climacteridae** (2/7) - Australo-Papuan treecreepers

Family **Menuridae** (2/4)

Subfamily **Menurinae** - lyrebirds

Subfamily **Atrichornithinae** - scrub-birds

Family **Ptilonorhynchidae** (7/20) - New Guinea bowerbirds

Superfamily **Meliphagoidea**

Family **Maluridae** (2/4)

Subfamily **Malurinae**

Tribe **Malurini** - fairywrens

Tribe **Stipiturini** - emuwrens

Subfamily **Amytornithinae** - grasswrens

Family **Meliphagidae** (42/182) - honeyeaters, Ephthianura, Ashbyia

Family **Pardalotidae** (16/68)

Subfamily **Pardalotinae** - pardalotes

Subfamily **Dasyornithinae** - bristlebirds

Subfamily **Acanthizinae**

Tribe **Sericornithini** - scrubwrens

Tribe **Acanthizini** - thornbills, whitefaces

Superfamily **Corvoidea**

Family **Eopsaltriidae** (14/46) - Australo-Papuan robins, Drymodes

Family **Irenidae** (2/10) - fairy-bluebirds, leaf birds

Family **Orthonychidae** (1/2) - logrunner, chowchilla

Family **Pomatostomidae** (1/5) - Australo-Papuan babblers

Family **Laniidae** (3/30) - true shrikes

Family **Vireonidae** (4/51) - vireos, greenlets, peppershrikes,
shrike-vireos

Family **Corvidae** (127/647)

Subfamily **Cinclosomatinae** - quail-thrushes, whipbirds

Subfamily **Corcoracinae** - Australian chough, apostlebird

Subfamily **Pachycephalinae**

Tribe **Neosittini** - sittellas

Tribe **Mohouini** - Mohoua, Finschia

Tribe **Falcunculini** - shrike-tits, Oreoica, Rhagologus

Tribe **Pachycephalini** - whistlers, shrike-thrushes

Subfamily **Corvinae**

Tribe **Corvini** - crows, magpies, jays, nutcrackers

Tribe **Paradisaeini** - birds-of-paradise, Melampitta

Tribe **Artamini** - currawongs, woodswallows

Tribe **Oriolini** - orioles, cuckooshrikes

Subfamily **Dicrurinae**

Tribe **Rhipidurini** - fantails

Tribe **Dicrurini** - drongos

Tribe **Monarchini** - monarchs, magpie-larks

Subfamily **Aegithininae** - Ioras

Subfamily **Malaconotinae**

    Tribe **Malaconotini** - bush-shrikes

    Tribe **Vangini** - helmet-shrikes, vangas, Batis, Platysteira

Family **Callaeatidae** (3/3) - New Zealand wattlebirds

Parvorder **Incertae sedis**

    Family **Picathartidae** - Picathartes, Chaetops

Parvorder **Passerida**

  Superfamily **Muscicapoidea**

    Family **Bombycillidae** (5/8)

      Tribe **Dulini** - palmchat

      Tribe **Ptilogonatini** - silky-flycatchers

      Tribe **Bombycillini** - waxwings

    Family **Cinclidae** (1/5) - dippers

    Family **Muscicapidae** (69/449)

     Subfamily **Turdinae** - true thrushes, Chlamydochaera

     Subfamily **Muscicapinae**

      Tribe **Muscicapini** - Old World flycatchers

      Tribe **Saxicolini** - chats

    Family **Sturnidae** (38/148)

      Tribe **Sturnini** - starlings, mynas

      Tribe **Mimini** - mockingbirds, thrashers, catbirds

  Superfamily **Sylvioidea**

    Family **Sittidae** (2/25)

     Subfamily **Sittinae** - nuthatches

     Subfamily **Tichodrominae** - wallcreeper

    Family **Certhiidae** (22/97)

     Subfamily **Certhiinae**

      Tribe **Certhiini** - northern creepers

      Tribe **Salpornithini** - African creeper

     Subfamily **Troglodytinae** - wrens

     Subfamily **Polioptilinae** - gnatcatchers, verdin, gnatwrens

    Family **Paridae** (7/65)

     Subfamily **Remizinae** - penduline-tits

     Subfamily **Parinae** - titmice, chickadees

    Family **Aegithalidae** (3/8) - long-tailed tits, bushtits

Family **Hirundinidae** (14/89)

  Subfamily **Pseudochelidoninae** - river-martins

  Subfamily **Hirundininae** - swallows, martins

Family **Regulidae** (1/6) - kinglets

Family **Pycnonotidae** (21/137) - bulbuls, greenbuls

Family **Hypocoliidae** (1/1) - Hypocolius

Family **Cisticolidae** (14/119) - African warblers, Cisticola, Apalis, Prinia

Family **Zosteropidae** (13/96) - white-eyes

Family **Sylviidae** (101/552)

  Subfamily **Acrocephalinae** - leaf-warblers

  Subfamily **Megalurinae** - grass-warblers

  Subfamily **Garrulacinae** - laughing thrushes

  Subfamily **Sylviinae**

    Tribe **Timaliini** - babblers, Rhabdoria

    Tribe **Chamaeini** - wrentit

    Tribe **Sylviini** - Sylvia

Superfamily **Passeroidea**

 Family **Alaudidae** (17/91) - larks

 Family **Nectariniidae** (8/169)

  Subfamily **Promeropinae** - sugarbirds

  Subfamily **Nectariniinae**

    Tribe **Dicaeini** - flowerpeckers

    Tribe **Nectariniini** - Sunbirds, spiderhunters

 Family **Melanocharitidae** (3/10)

    Tribe **Melanocharitini** - Melanocharis

    Tribe **Toxorhamphini** - Toxorhamphus, Oedistoma

 Family **Paramythiidae** (2/2) - Paramythia, Oreocharis

 Family **Passeridae** (57/386)

  Subfamily **Passerinae** - sparrows, rock-sparrows

  Subfamily **Motacillinae** - wagtails, pipits

  Subfamily **Prunellinae** - accentors, dunnock

  Subfamily **Ploceinae** - weavers

  Subfamily **Estrildinae**

    Tribe **Estrildini** - estrildine finches

    Tribe **Viduini** - whydahs

Family **Fringillidae** (240/993)

  Subfamily **Peucedraminae** - Peucedramus

  Subfamily **Fringillinae**

    Tribe **Fringillini** - chaffinches, brambling

    Tribe **Carduelini** - goldfinches, crossbills

    Tribe **Drepanidini** - Hawaiian honeycreepers

  Subfamily **Emberizinae**

    Tribe **Emberizini** - buntings, longspurs, towhees

    Tribe **Parulini** - wood warblers, Zeledonia

    Tribe **Thraupini** - tanagers, Neotropical honeycreepers,
      seedeaters, flower-piercers

    Tribe **Cardinalini** - cardinals

    Tribe **Icterini** - troupials, New World blackbirds,
      meadowlarks